Faith Leadership in a Divided Culture

The Religious Freedom Debates—and Why They Matter to All of Us

ISBN: 978-1-945269-31-8

Funding for this research was made possible by the generous support of Maclellan Family Foundations (Chattanooga, TN) as part of their First Freedom Project initiative. Barna Group was solely responsible for data collection, analysis and writing of the report.

Table of Contents

Introduction

Several years ago, a well-known restaurant chain produced a video to use as part of new employee training. They wanted the video to remind their employees of a simple fact: Every person who came into one of their restaurants was a human being first and a customer second. Panning over the various people in the story, the camera would sometimes pause and linger over one person as words were superimposed next to them describing the circumstances of that person's life—facing unemployment, depression, the loss of a loved one or, alternatively, the welcome news they had beaten cancer or had recently received a college scholarship. As this video reminded trainees, we encounter people in ignorance every day, having no idea what challenges they face or what blessings they have been given. These same people are, nonetheless, made in the divine image and *do* have a story, even if we do not know it. "You have never met a mere mortal," C. S. Lewis once said.

Of course, when someone points this out to us, the hope is often that this fact would drive us toward our neighbors, that it would help us to see them with affection, that it would motivate us to treat them gently and, ultimately, that it would cause us to love them. Actually remembering that is difficult at times. Indeed, there may be few societies where it is *more* difficult than our own. Twitter feeds, Facebook timelines, hashtags, memes and the ease of disembodied arguments make it easier than ever to see our neighbors as Other—without ever meeting one another, we can shout #MAGA and #NeverTrump and #FakeNews. We don't know the stories of the people at the other end of our social media political tirades. As many news reports, pundits and cultural commentators have noted, we are facing a crisis of neighborliness in the United States—namely, that we don't know (or, often, trust) our neighbors. This makes it challenging to remember that every person we meet has a story, that they are significant, that they are beloved by God. Yet that is precisely what Christians are called to do. How can we fulfill this call in a world that makes loving one's neighbor so difficult?

In this report we talk about the tribal nature of the US today, the ways in which we have grown apart from one another and separated ourselves into ever smaller subgroups. In a tribalized context, we do not see our fellow man or woman as an image-bearer of God facing great challenges, but only as a person so identified with the label we have assigned to them that they may as well be wearing it on their T-shirt. "Black." "White." "Liberal." "Conservative." "Gay." "Straight." In such a world, the response Christianity can offer is that of Holy Spirit-empowered neighborliness and love. But unfortunately, the nature of our polarization is that even claims of love are not self-evident to us. What one person regards as demonstrating love looks to another like something quite different.

In a tribalized context, we do not see our fellow man or woman as an image-bearer facing great challenges

As a result, two issues we often see as separate actually appear to be quite closely related. The first, how Christians can show love to their neighbors in a fragmenting world, is tied to the second: how we should understand issues of religious liberty and the freedom of individual people to practice their religion as they see fit. In other words, how can we hold firm to our convictions and beliefs, both in deed and word, and still hold space for relationships and civility with those who believe differently than us? Can religious freedom and religious plurality peacefully coexist?

We can break these questions down even further. Here are five lenses through which we can look at these issues, as described by David Kinnaman and Gabe Lyons in their 2017 book *Good Faith*:

How can we hold firm to our convictions and beliefs, both in deed and word, and still hold space for relationships and civility with those who believe differently than us?

Theology: What do God's Word and the Church's wisdom reveal about this?

Ministry: What is the proper pastoral response to people living in a fallen world?

Relationships: How should I engage friends and neighbors with whom I disagree?

Politics: What government policies, however imperfect, best empower human flourishing?

Public Square: What is the appropriate relationship between personal conviction and day-to-day interactions with those who hold different beliefs?

Introducing these five different themes can help us make the distinctions we need to make when facing a hard social or political problem. By making these distinctions we can recognize that there are different perspectives from which politicians, business owners, pastors and lay Christians might validly answer questions about religious liberty. Moreover, because each of these five lenses is rooted in a Christian concern related to the love of God and love of neighbor, they provide us with a guide for answering questions about religious liberty in ways that help us to love our neighbors well without violating conscience or disobeying the commands given in scripture. Through

Introducing these five different themes can help us make the distinctions we need to make when facing a hard political problem

the rest of this book, you'll notice these icons in the margins, indicating when we're looking at the issues through one of these lenses.

In 2014, Barna surveyed faith leaders, Christian and otherwise, to learn how they viewed the present state and the future prospects of religious freedom in America. This two-year national study among US clergy comprised of random, representative interviews with 1,963 evangelical Protestant, mainline Protestant and Catholic pastors, as well as clergy outside of the Christian tradition, including Jewish, Muslim, Hindu, Mormon and other faith leaders, is the backbone of this report. We also interviewed an over-representative sample of African American Protestant pastors. (Throughout this report, "faith leaders" and "US clergy" refer to religious leaders of all faith traditions while "pastors" refers to Christian leaders alone. You can find a complete methodology of the research and a glossary of terms in the Appendix). The following year, 2015, was notable for a number of events that had potential consequences for religious freedom, so Barna repeated the 2014 survey in 2015, 2016 and 2017 to discern whether the controversy surrounding these events, as well as various political shifts that occurred in those years, affected faith leaders' views about religious freedom in the US.

This report is the culmination of Barna's four years of research examining faith leaders' views on matters of religious liberty. It includes research primarily from Barna, supplemented by data from additional studies to frame current issues and events. Its primary focus is on how Christian pastors and other faith leaders perceive challenges and opportunities related to cultural trends and their impact on religious freedom, but also included are findings from research among the general US population for comparison and context. Taken together, the data represent the broadest study Barna has yet undertaken on the ways faith in general and Christianity in particular are perceived, expressed and limited in the public square.

The goal for this report is threefold: 1) to offer accurate insights about the views of US faith leaders and adults on current issues, 2) to frame the context into which these findings fit and 3) to generate a range of questions and ideas that can inform the faith community's response.

Whether you are a clergy member or lead in another sphere of American life, we invite you to listen to the concerns of a critical segment of cultural leaders on the state of religious liberty and to evaluate their ideas about leading people of faith into an uncertain future.

Faith Leadership in a Divided Culture tours a range of Barna's findings, but several key themes emerge from the research:

This report is the culmination of Barna's four years of research examining faith leaders' views on matters of religious liberty

- Faith leaders, especially pastors, are concerned that religious freedom is under threat, or at least undergoing significant redefinition. These perceptions are especially intense among non-mainline Protestant, black Protestant and Catholic leaders, but are less so among mainline Protestant and non-Christian clergy (though a majority in every segment expresses at least some level of concern).

- The LGBT community and same-sex rights are at the heart of today's religious freedom debates and the primary concern for clergy. Though most clergy feel as though legal same-sex marriage was inevitable, they are committed to actively resisting and reversing it while defending their right to refuse performing same-sex weddings. Overall, they feel somewhat prepared to address a number of LGBT-related issues, but are skeptical of the possibility of advancing LGBT rights while protecting religious freedom, viewing them as mostly incompatible objectives.

In the debates over religious freedom, both sides seem to be entrenching

- In the debates over religious freedom, both sides seem to be entrenching. Pastors and the general public are moving increasingly toward group solidarity in response to mounting uncertainty about religious freedom. Most Americans believe that no one set of values should dominate the country but, paradoxically, a growing number want preference for their own set of values—leading to tribalistic tendencies and potentially deeper divisions.

- While the outcomes of Americans' religious freedom debates will certainly affect every church, the issue isn't a top concern for most pastors. Pastors admit they are more concerned with the morality of America and declining church attendance. They also identify a diminishment of their own influence. This points to a concern for the broader secularizing trends of which religious freedom is but a subset.

- Faith leaders want to be part of the solution to the problems facing a religiously plural and increasingly secular society. They believe people in their congregations are looking for wisdom and direction when it comes to complicated social issues, and most say clergy have a special calling to guide people across tricky cultural terrain.

- Faith leaders are under pressure and are often unclear about how best to lead. They feel pressured both to speak and not to speak on the issues and, while they want to help, many seem either overconfident in their readiness or hyper-concerned about negative reactions they might garner both inside and outside their fellowship.

Overall, as we will see, there is a sense among faith leaders that society is drawing heavier lines around free religious expression in the public square. As leaders they want to help define where those lines are drawn, but many, despite their best efforts at fruitful cultural engagement, see the lines becoming less porous and hemming in people of faith further from public life. Yet most also feel hopeful that they are uniquely positioned to help their community of faith find sure footing in the days ahead, no matter where the lines are drawn—if only they knew how. Barna hopes the insights in this report will help leaders renew their confidence to lead well in these divided times.

Definitions

US adults are US residents 18 and older. (Find an extended glossary of Barna terms referring to segments of US adults in the Appendix.)

US clergy members are leaders in Christian, Jewish, Muslim, Hindu and other religious traditions. They are also referred to as "faith leaders" or just "clergy."

Non-Christian clergy are leaders in religious traditions other than mainstream Christianity.

Christian clergy are pastors of a congregation in a mainstream tradition of Christianity.

Protestant clergy are pastors of a congregation in a Protestant tradition of Christianity.

- **Mainline clergy** pastor in denominations such as as American Baptist Churches USA, the Episcopal Church, Evangelical Lutheran Church of America, United Church of Christ, United Methodist Church and Presbyterian Church USA.
- **Non-mainline clergy** pastor in denominations such as charismatic / Pentecostal churches, the Southern Baptist Convention, churches in the Wesleyan-Holiness tradition and nondenominational churches.

Catholic clergy pastor a Catholic parish.

African American Protestant pastors are Protestant clergy who lead congregations that are majority black. Barna recruited a robust oversample of these leaders in order to analyze how their views and experiences may be different from the national average.

Key Findings

- Three-quarters of US clergy members believe religious freedom is becoming less valued. Two out of five US adults say religious freedom is worse than 10 years ago (43%).

3/4

- Nearly half of US faith leaders predict that other freedoms, in addition to religious liberty, will be at risk in the coming decade (44%).

<1/2

- More than two-thirds of Christian pastors (69%) would like Judeo-Christian values to be given preference in the US. The same proportion of non-Christian clergy wants no single set of values to be given preference.

2/3

- Most clergy members feel at least somewhat prepared to teach their congregants how to engage constructively on sensitive social issues (93%). However, only seven percent would say their congregants are very well equipped to do so right now.

7%

- Potential limitations on religious freedom are a concern for faith leaders (54%), but concerns about young people dropping out of church (72%) and the decline of the traditional family (65%) are even more widespread.

>1/2

- Now that same-sex marriage is legal across the country, more than nine out of 10 clergy insist religious groups must remain free to teach and practice a traditional definition of marriage (92%). Eight out of 10 US adults agree (79%).

9/10

The United State of Religious Liberty

Clergy in the US generally agree on issues around religious liberty: most are concerned about the future of religious freedom, yet few would identify it as one of their top ministry priorities.

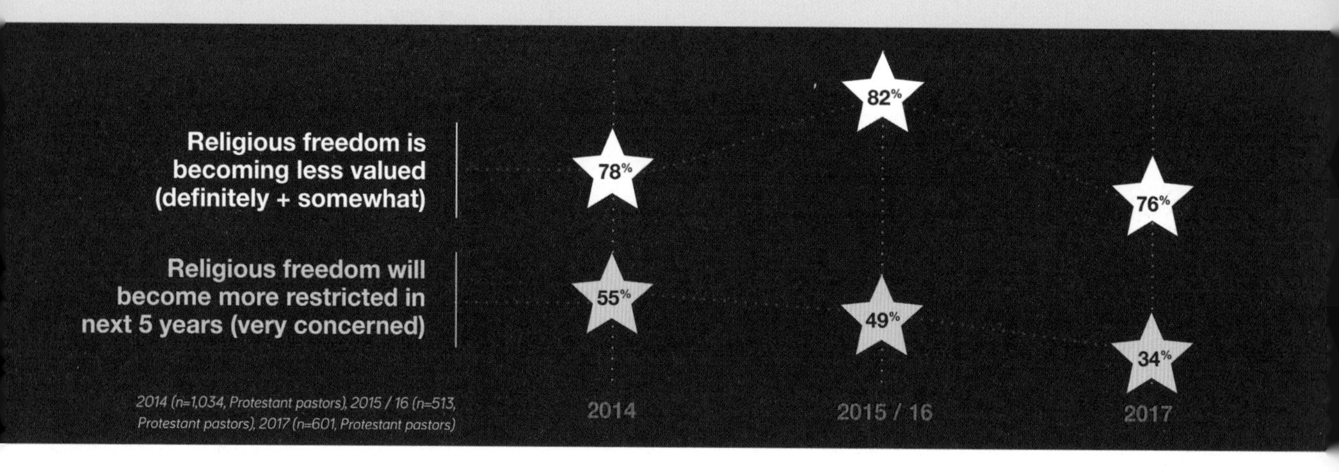

What Defines the Common Standard for Moral Values in the US?

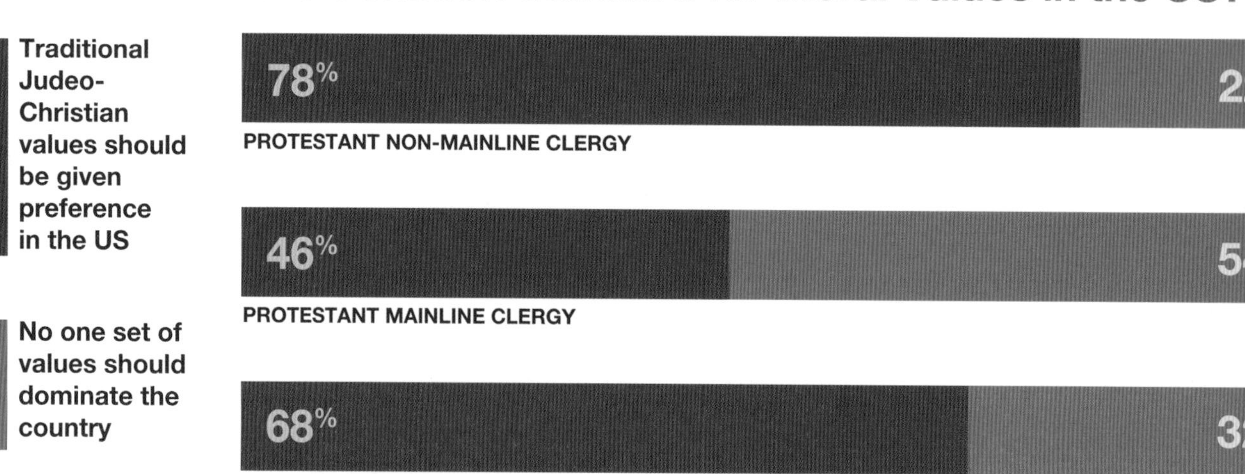

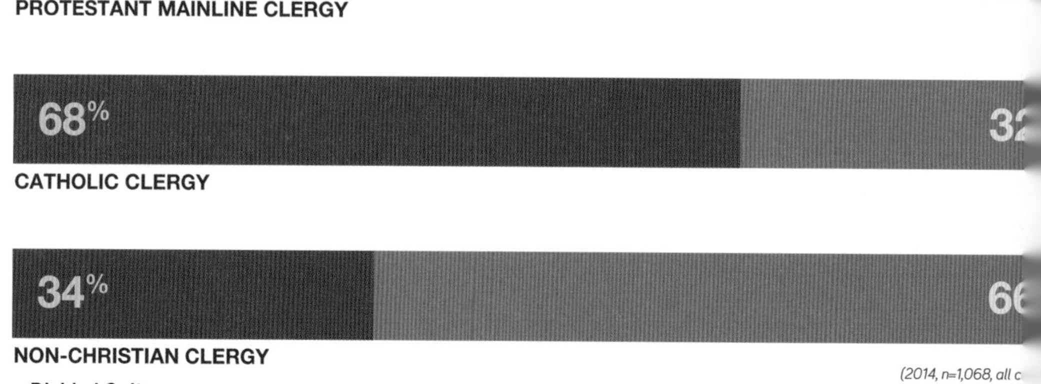

(2014, n=1,068, all c

89% of clergy are motivated to learn more about religious liberty in the next year (definitely + probably)

(2014, n=1,608, all clergy)

87% of clergy say the US is a religiously plural nation (86% identify the country as "a nation in transition spiritually")

(2014, n=1,608, all clergy)

82% of clergy define religious liberty as "the freedom to practice religion without interference from government"

(2014, n=1,608, all clergy)

78% of clergy identify religious extremists from non-Christian traditions as negatively impacting religious freedom (75% point to influence of atheism and 70% to Christian religious extremists)

(2014, n=725, all clergy)

68% of clergy say they have a uniquely important role to play when it comes to preserving religious freedom in the US

(2014, n=1,608, all clergy)

72% of clergy say they are likely to work with a local clergyperson of another faith on issues of religious liberty in the next year (definitely + probably)

(2014, n=1,608, all clergy)

54% of clergy are very concerned limitations on freedom of religion will affect their ministry in the next decade

(2014, n=812, all clergy)

Chapter 1

The Role of Religious Freedom in a Pluralistic Culture

Americans have always disagreed about the practices of religious belief. In 17th-century New England, the free-thinking Roger Williams challenged the Puritan leaders of the Massachusetts Bay Colony for restricting what Williams called "soul freedom," by which he meant the right for an individual soul to worship God as he or she saw fit without interference from other parties. The Puritans, led by a pastor named John Cotton, argued against Williams, saying that the people needed to remain united in their walk with Christ and that introducing division on matters of personal belief would jeopardize the life of the community. The dispute turned out to be irresolvable, with Williams contending earnestly for the freedom of the individual person to practice their faith, and Cotton insisting on the necessity of unity in the Body of Christ. The debate "ended" with Williams being banished from Massachusetts and settling in a new part of New England that would become the colony of Rhode Island, an eventual haven for religious dissidents.

Even in its earliest days, America was a place riven by debates over religious liberty, with communities quite literally fracturing and beginning anew over the issue. Though we are today arguing about issues like same-sex marriage and employer-provided healthcare, the underlying question—how do we balance the individual's liberty to practice their religious beliefs freely with the need to maintain a coherent common life for all Americans?—is still a part of our life in the United States.

How do we balance the individual's liberty to practice their religious beliefs freely with the need to maintain a coherent common life for all Americans?

Indeed, we are still using many of the same *terms* that were first used 350 years ago! Today, Russell Moore, president of the Southern Baptist Convention's Ethics and Religious Liberty Commission, often uses the term "soul freedom" when arguing for religious liberty.[1] In this sense, the question of what role religious belief should play in public life is not at all new. Indeed, it is older than the United States itself. Yet new questions are being asked as successive generations are less connected to Christianity—or to religion at all—and America moves into the post-Christian future. Both the common good and the Church's testimony call for careful thought about this issue.

One of the foremost challenges to careful thought concerning these questions is that public awareness of these debates is mixed—even among clergy. This chapter explores how pastors and the general public define terms related to religious freedom and how they view the religious landscape of the United States.

- Is America considered a Christian nation, or do most people believe we live in a religiously plural or secular context?
- Is there broad agreement across denominational and faith segments?

This chapter also examines how clergy and adults overall view changing attitudes toward religious freedom in America and how these views have changed over time.

- Has religious freedom become more restricted?
- What is the level of concern among pastors and the general population about religious freedom?

Defining Religious Freedom

When it comes to defining terms on religious freedom, there is little confusion. Most religious leaders prefer a definition that mirrors the language of the First Amendment: that the government shall not prohibit the free exercise of religion. In the 2014 survey of all Christian and non-Christian clergy, over eight in 10 (82%) said that religious liberty is "freedom to practice religion without interference from government." Far fewer defined it as "the freedom from laws and policies that favor one religion over another" (8%) or "the freedom to make personal choices without interference from religious organizations" (7%).

These numbers hold true for most segments, but non-Christian clergy (58%) were less likely to choose the majority definition, when compared to Catholic (90%) and Protestant non-mainline clergy (88%). They are more likely than other clergy segments to say that religious liberty is either "freedom from laws and policies that favor one religion over another" or "the freedom to make personal choices without interference from religious organizations" than almost any other group. As minorities, non-Christian clergy are likely more willing to embrace government oversight or intervention to ensure freedom of conscience and equal protection, in light of an influential Christian majority. Among Protestant denominations, African American clergy (69%) are also slightly less convinced of this top choice, perhaps also the result of a minority experience.

The Best Definition of Religious Freedom

% among US faith leaders

- The freedom to practice religion without interference from government
- The freedom from laws and policies that favor one religion over another
- The freedom to make personal choices without interference from religious organizations

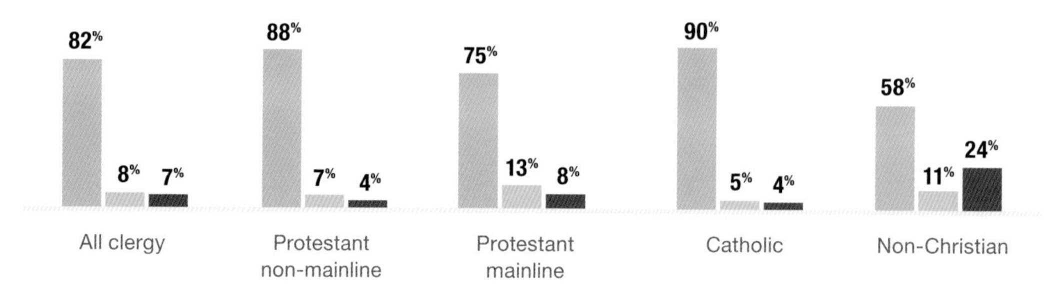

(2014 n=1,608)

When it comes to the general public, a majority of American adults affirm a similar definition: "True religious freedom means that all citizens must have freedom of conscience, which means being able to believe and practice the core commitments and values of your faith."

However, over the past five years, consensus around this definition has begun to break down. In 2012, 69 percent of Americans favored the definition, but by 2017 that number had fallen to 55 percent. Though most still agree (at least somewhat), it appears American adults are feeling less certain about this definition. The same is true for practicing Christians, who have seen a similar decline from 78 percent in 2012 to 62 percent in 2017. In light of recent public battles over religious freedom and increasing hostility toward traditional views, Americans appear less willing to defend the right for religious Americans to believe and practice the core commitments and values of their faith, particularly when affirming religious freedom of this sort also means that minority groups may be discriminated against in some way.

Over the past five years, consensus around the definition of religious liberty has begun to break down

US Adults on What Religious Freedom Means, 2012 to 2017

"True religious freedom means that all citizens must have freedom of conscience, which means being able to believe and practice the core commitments and values of your faith."

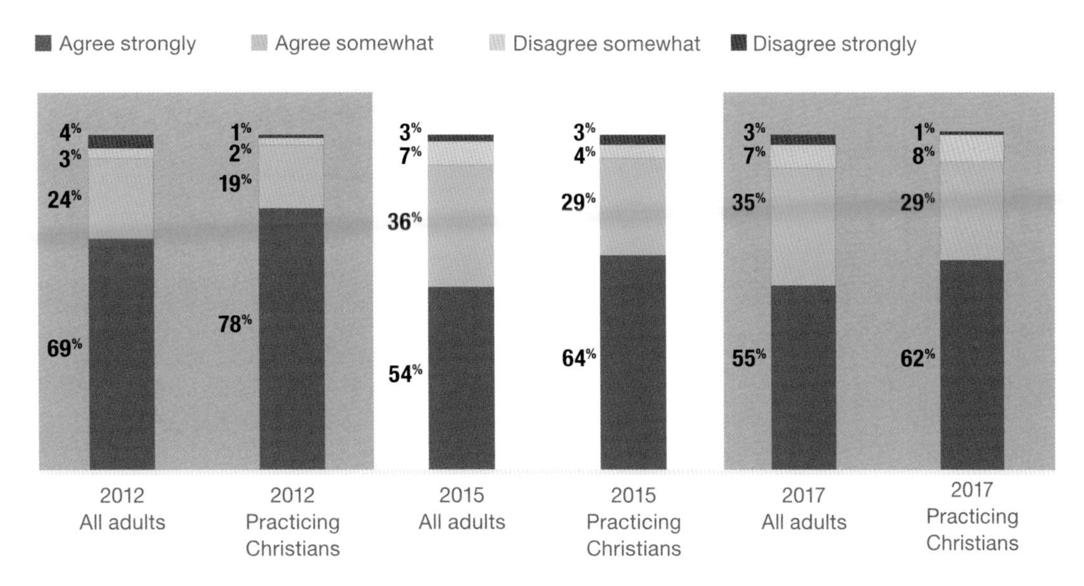

(Gen Pop: 2012 | n=1,008, 2015 | n=1,005 , 2017, n=1,019)

Religious Descriptions of the US

One significant explanation for the shift in how Americans view religious liberty is, of course, the broader shifts in the religious lives of many Americans. Though Americans struggle to agree on the importance of religious liberty, they do generally agree that religious identity in the United States is changing. More than half of those surveyed, and more than 80 percent of faith leaders, describe the US as "a religiously plural nation" and "a nation in transition spiritually."

Viewed through a relationship lens, then, one of the main questions confronting many Americans is how to live well with neighbors who are very different. How do we build bonds of neighborliness across religious, class, ethnic, racial and linguistic lines?

Though Americans struggle to agree on the importance of religious liberty, they do generally agree that religious identity in the United States is changing

While most clergy agree America is in a period of religious transition, impressions of where the country *is* in that transition diverge along faith lines. Non-Christian clergy (58%) are less likely than all faith leaders (73%) to agree that "a secular nation" is an accurate description, possibly because more than two in five of them (43%) still see the United States as "a Christian nation." At the other end of the spectrum, 79 percent of Protestant non-mainline clergy describe the nation as "secular," as do 72 percent of Catholic clergy and 66 percent of Protestant mainline clergy. About one in five Protestant non-mainline clergy (21%) and mainline clergy (18%) would say the United States is currently "a Christian nation."

The outliers among Christian clergy are Catholics, nearly half of whom (49%) say the nation is still Christian. One plausible explanation is that Catholics were for many years excluded from mainstream America. It was only during the post–World War II years that American Catholics began to be seen as mainstream Americans; Bishop Fulton Sheen's TV shows and President John F. Kennedy's political success were two major factors in this shift. Given how long it took Catholics to gain such standing in Christian America, it is perhaps unsurprising that they are reluctant to regard America as *not* being a Christian nation. If America is not Christian, does that once again push Catholics outside the American mainstream?

That exception aside, the pattern is striking: Christians see the nation as transitioning away from Christianity while non-Christians identify the US as strongly religious. Where do these diverging responses come from?

One possibility is that, as America becomes more polarized, both "sides" of the divide feel their position is under threat because of the extremism of their ideological opposites. A second contributing factor is that, as local communities become less influential and the centralized power of the federal government becomes larger, a great deal of one's day-to-day life can be shaped by the decisions of the president and the Supreme Court.

These anxieties were on display during the 2016 US presidential campaign. Some Christians worried a Hillary Clinton victory would mean Christian business owners could face large fines or even arrest if they refused to comply with laws that violate their conscience. Meanwhile, Donald Trump's call for a ban on Muslim immigration provoked concern that ethnic or religious minority communities would be treated unfairly under his presidency. Regardless of who won, there were plausible reasons for both sides to worry about their religious liberties changing in a major way as a result of political events.

Christians see the nation as transitioning away from Christianity while non-Christians identify the US as strongly religious

How to Understand Religion in the US Today (Part 1)

% "accurate" among US faith leaders

	All clergy	Protestant non-mainline	Protestant mainline	Catholic	Non-Christian
A religiously plural nation	87%	86%	89%	86%	89%
A nation in transition spiritually	86%	86%	88%	85%	85%
A secular nation	73%	79%	66%	72%	58%
A post-Christian nation	61%	68%	65%	37%	35%
A Christian nation	26%	21%	18%	49%	43%

(2014, n=1,608)

Half of the American public believes the US is still a Christian nation, compared to only one-quarter of all clergy

Moving from clergy to US adults overall, the picture shifts slightly. In a survey conducted in 2015, two-thirds of US adults agreed that America is "a religiously plural nation." Over half (53%) also said that "a nation in transition spiritually" is an accurate description. That said, the general population is much more equivocal in their assessment of the nation's religious identity. Half of the American public (49%) still believes the US is a Christian nation, compared to only one-quarter of all clergy (26%). The general population is also much less likely to believe the US is a secular nation. While 73 percent of all faith leaders and 79 percent of non-mainline Protestant clergy say the nation is secular, only 43 percent of all US adults believe the United States is a secular nation.

The research does not provide an explanation for these different views between clergy and the general population. Pastors have had a front-row seat for the well-documented decline in church attendance and affiliation that has occurred in recent decades, and thus may

How to Understand Religion in the US Today (Part 2)

% among US faith leaders and US adults 18 and older

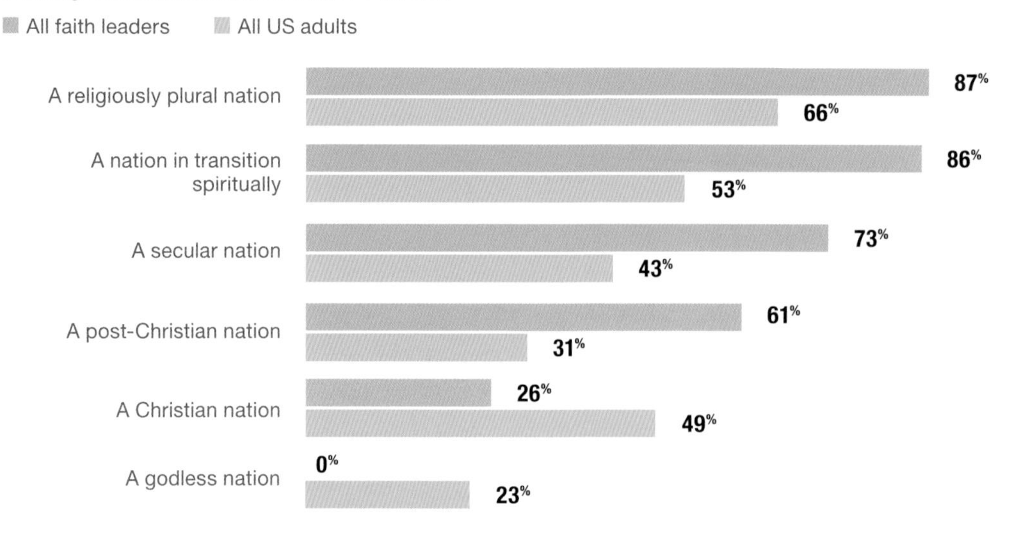

Good Faith: 2015 US Adults (*n*=1,000) • 2014 Clergy (*n*=1,608)

perceive changes that are not apparent to others. On the other hand, the emotional and professional investment that clergy have in the religious lives of Americans may cause them to exaggerate the changes they see.

Value of Religious Freedom in the US

In light of the religious shifts they perceive in America, do clergy believe religious freedom is declining? Most, regardless of religious affiliation, say religious freedom is less valued and less protected than in the past. In the 2014 study of Christian and non-Christian faith leaders, half said that it is *definitely* becoming less valued. Another one-quarter (24%) believed it is becoming *somewhat* less valued. While mainline Protestants were less likely than other Christian clergy to say religious freedom is becoming *definitely* (29%) or *somewhat* (25%) less valued, together these views still comprised a majority opinion (54%). Non-mainline Protestants were more unequivocal (62%) in their belief that the value of religious freedom is *definitely* diminishing, while somewhat fewer Catholics (45%) said so.

Most clergy, regardless of religious affiliation, perceive that religious freedom is less valued and less protected than in the past

Non-Christian faith leaders in 2014 also perceived a diminishing appreciation for religious freedom in the US. One-third (34%) said it is definitely less valued today and another one in five (22%) said it is somewhat less valued. Compared to Christian pastors overall, they were also more likely to say religious freedom is alive and well (44% somewhat and definitely), along with slightly less than half of mainline Protestants (46%).

In 2014, a religious liberty lawsuit involving popular retailer Hobby Lobby went all the way to the Supreme Court. In 2016, a case involving the Catholic religious order The Little Sisters of the Poor similarly went to the nation's highest court. Both cases concerned sections of the Affordable Care Act, which requires employers to provide various forms of contraception, some of which may be abortifacients, as part of their healthcare benefits package. Catholic charities and a number of other faith-based adoption agencies were compelled to abandon their services in Boston and Washington, D.C., for their refusal to place children with same-sex parents. In addition, photographers, florists and owners of bakeries and bed-and-breakfasts became subject to state and local sanctions (or even prosecution) for refusing to offer services for same-sex marriage ceremonies. Faith-based educational institutions also feared losing their tax-exempt status over challenges to their beliefs about sexuality, gender and marriage, leading to a great deal of uncertainty about the future of religious freedom in the US.

Most of these cases have been decided in favor of religious organizations and businesses, but it may be that the experience of being adjudicated rather than simply assumed has left clergy questioning the future of religious liberty in the United States.

The Cultural Value of Religious Freedom

% among US faith leaders; "Religious freedom is..."

	All clergy	Protestant non-mainline	Protestant mainline	Catholic	Non-Christian
Definitely becoming less valued	**50%**	**62%**	**29%**	**45%**	**34%**
Somewhat becoming less valued	**24%**	**23%**	**25%**	**26%**	**22%**
Somewhat alive and well	**14%**	**9%**	**23%**	**13%**	**25%**
Definitely alive and well	**12%**	**7%**	**23%**	**17%**	**19%**

(2014, n=1,608)

Shifts in the Value of Religious Freedom

Between the initial study in 2014 and subsequent surveys in 2015 to 2017, these perceptions have changed somewhat. Among Protestant clergy, those who claim that religious freedom is definitely becoming less valued dropped 11 percentage points from 55 percent to 44 percent. Those who said it was somewhat less valued increased nine percentage points from 23 percent in 2014 to 32 percent in 2017.

The success of high-profile cases such as the one brought by Hobby Lobby, as well President Trump's promises to promote and protect religious freedom, may have eased concerns among religious leaders, explaining some of the movement in the data. Over the same period, the minority view that religious liberty is at least somewhat alive and well remained the same (23%), but became less certain (11% definitely in 2014 vs. 6% in 2017). The concerns of Protestant clergy about religious freedom are easing—but not vanishing. Among both the majority who believe it is becoming less valued and the cautiously optimistic minority a great deal of uncertainty remains.

The concerns of Protestant clergy about religious freedom are easing—but not vanishing

The Cultural Value of Religious Freedom, 2014 to 2017

% among Protestant pastors

Somewhat becoming less valued
Definitely becoming less valued

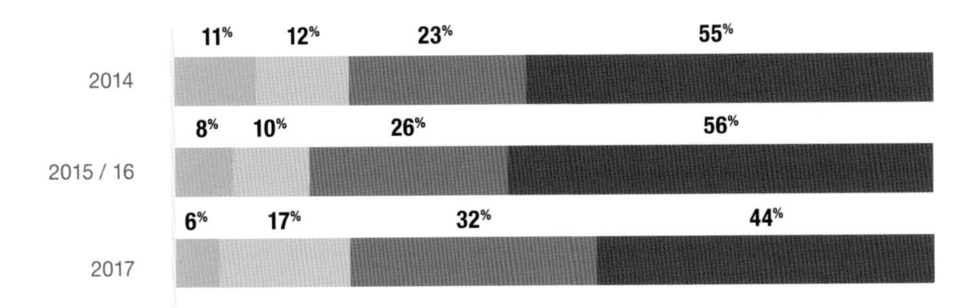

Pastor data: 2014 (n=1,038), 2015 / 16 (n=513), 2017 (n=601)

The general US population also sees the value of religious freedom decreasing. When asked in 2012 if they believe that freedom of religion in the US is worse, better or about the same as it was 10 years before, most said freedom of religion was about the same as it was 10 years ago (42%), while only one-third (33%) said it was worse. This essentially flipped in 2015, when one-third reported it was the same, while four in 10 said worse (41%). That trend continued into 2017, with 43 percent saying it had become worse and fewer saying it was the same (27%).

In other words, the belief that religious freedom in the US is on the decline *increased* by 10 percentage points over the course of five years. Although the successes of religious liberty cases in recent years have likely eased concerns among clergy, concern among US adults appears to be growing—even though their level of concern currently matches clergy. The Supreme Court's decision in *Obergefell vs. Hodges* to legalize same-sex marriage in all 50 states caused particular concern that individuals and churches, as Justice Clarence Thomas commented, might be "confronted with demands to participate in and endorse civil marriages between same-sex couples."

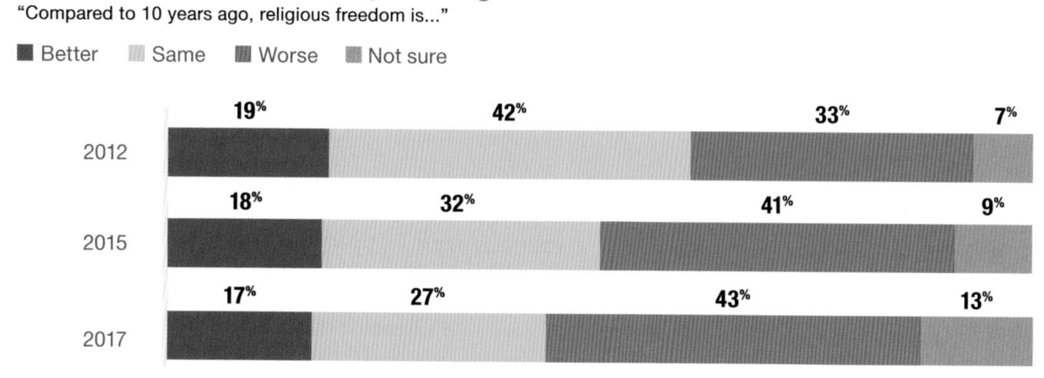

Gen pop: 2012 (n=1,008), 2015 (n=1,200), 2017 (n=1,019)

These demands have played out very publicly. For example, Kentucky County Clerk Kim Davis, who, because of her beliefs about marriage, refused to issue a marriage license to a same-sex couple after the *Obergefell* decision, was sued by the American Civil Liberties Union and ordered by a federal judge to issue the license. After an unsuccessful appeal, she continued to refuse to issue licenses and was subsequently jailed for contempt of court. This and other cases like it have likely contributed to growing concern in recent years.

Future Threats to Religious Freedom

A plurality of Americans believe freedom of religion in the US is worse than it was 10 years ago, and most clergy believe it is becoming less valued—so what do they envision for the future?

In the 2014 survey, over half of Protestant pastors (55%) admitted they were *very* concerned that religious freedom will become more restricted in the next five years. This dropped to below half in the 2015 / 2016 study, and to one-third (34%) in 2017.

Americans believe freedom of religion in the US is worse than it was 10 years ago, and clergy believe it is becoming less valued

In many ways, these decreasing concerns belie the realities on the ground and in the headlines during these years. In 2015, in particular, several high-profile religious liberty stories dominated the news, including the controversial passage (and amendment) of the Indiana Religious Freedom Restoration Act, which proponents claimed was intended to restrict government's ability to infringe on religious rights; the landmark ruling in *Obergefell vs. Hodges* in the Supreme Court, granting marriage rights to same-sex couples; and threats to repeal the accreditation of Gordon College for their statement of faith on marriage as limited to a man and a woman. These controversies were national news, yet most pastors concerns about religious freedom *decreased* during those years—perhaps indicating less of a "headline sensitivity" than one might expect.

That said, most pastors are not moving from *very concerned* to a total lack of concern. Most clergy shifting away from very concerned have simply moved to *somewhat* concerned, which increased from one-quarter (25%) in 2014 to 31 percent in 2015 / 16, to two in five (39%) in 2017. Pastors who said they were not too concerned about future restrictions of religious freedom increased from one in eight (12%) in 2014 to one in five (20%) in 2017.

Concern that Religious Freedom Will Become More Restricted in the Next Five Years, 2014 to 2017

% among US Protestant pastors

	2014	2015 / 16	2017
Very concerned	55%	49%	34%
Somewhat concerned	25%	31%	39%
Not too concerned	12%	12%	20%
Not at all concerned	8%	8%	7%

Pastor data: 2014 (*n*=1,050), 2015/16 (*n*=512), 2017 (*n*=601)

A Broader Context for the Religious Liberty Debates

As we have explored, contention over religious liberty has been part of America since the 1600s. That we are still divided on these questions in 2018 is not surprising. That said, the shift in how the general public thinks about same-sex marriage has introduced a new complicating factor that has contributed to growing fears about religious liberty among clergy, growing hostility to it among non-religious Americans, and no small amount of controversy about the place of religion in public life.

In the next chapter, we zoom out to look at the broader cultural context and the increased tribalism that defines public life in America. The challenge facing us is not only that we fight over religious liberty; it's that there is not much of a "we" in the United States today. Due to the fracturing of local communities, rising mistrust and loneliness, and a polarized political system, the common life of the United States is beginning to fray.

Contention over religious liberty has been a part of life in America since the 1600s

It is simply a fact that we are now a pluralistic country. But how to live well within our pluralism is a problem we have yet to resolve. The issue of religious liberty is less a unique, stand-alone issue that reflects animosity toward Christians and is instead part of a larger failure of community in the United States.

Chapter 2

The Effects of Tribalism

Americans have been lonely for a long time. In 1995 Harvard sociologist Robert Putnam published a paper called "Bowling Alone." Several years later, it would be expanded and published in book form.[2] In it, Putnam wrote of the decline of membership in various communities that have traditionally been a staple of American life. This included churches, but also things like the Rotary Club or bowling leagues—which inspired the title. He warned that America's "social capital"—the various "soft" benefits people enjoy when they are in close community with other people—is in decline.

Social capital is accrued through simple acts—borrowing a cup of sugar from a neighbor or chaperoning a school field trip—that bring us into contact with the people in our communities, weaving strands of familiarity into a web of connectedness. When this web begins to fall apart, society suffers. In 2015, for example, one in five Americans told Barna they regularly or often feel lonely. In a separate 2017 survey, just one in four Americans said they had managed to become friends with one or two of their neighbors.

This is why viewing religious liberty issues through a lens of relationship is so important. Our conversation around the issue is taking place in this context of increasing isolation and alienation. Absent the community bonds that social capital creates and the empathy it fosters, it is all too easy to perceive others as truly Other—to view difference as *danger*, the strange as *suspicious*, the unknown as *a threat*. The result, as we consider the debates over religious freedom, is that both sides seem to be digging in.

This chapter explores how pastors and the general public are moving toward group solidarity in response to mounting uncertainty about religious freedom. It addresses questions about the intersection of group identity, loneliness and religious liberty in the United States.

Our conversation around religious liberty is taking place in a context of increasing isolation and alienation

- How can we build strong communities of faith marked by real solidarity with one another without also inadvertently adopting more tribalistic vices?
- Most Americans believe that no one set of values should dominate the country, but a growing number want preference for their own set of values. Will these tribalistic tendencies produce deeper divisions?

This chapter also examines data on difficult conversations and the importance of friendships with those who are different.

The Rise of Tribalism

In the past decade, the word "tribalism" has become ubiquitous in American public discourse. Commentators have argued that tribalism, and the mentality it engenders, were critical in President Trump's 2016 election. It is the driving force of much of today's identity politics—a strong tendency to want to belong to, and identify with, a group of people who are like you. In a world marked by so much loneliness, it is inevitable that people will seek out communities that look and believe as they do. Group solidarity can be a good thing. It can lead to mobilization, to action, to survival. However, in an increasingly pluralistic society, it can also create deep divisions and an "us vs. them" mentality. It leads to echo chambers, ideological stubbornness and a vulnerability to subjective thinking.

The changing demographics of the United States are at the root of many of these anxieties and fierce divides, as we see in the data. More than 84 percent of adults told Barna in July 2015 that they agree with the statement, "There is a lot of anger and hostility between the different ethnic and racial groups in America today." The lack of a shared identity that can bridge growing ethnic, cultural, religious and economic divides is a very real challenge to resolving a contentious question like setting the boundary between freedom of conscience and the requirements of law.

In a world marked by loneliness, it is inevitable that people will seek out communities that look and believe as they do

How are clergy doing in this regard? When they were asked in 2014 about their preference for what should be the common standard for moral values in America, they tended to choose their own, showing a pronounced preference for the group to which they belong. Respondents were offered two options: "Traditional Judeo-Christian values should be given preference in the US" and "No one set of values should dominate the country." Two-thirds of US clergy (66%) chose the former over the latter (34%). Protestant non-mainline clergy (78%) were the most likely to prefer the first option, along with seven in 10 Catholics (68%). Fewer than half of mainline Protestants (46%) and just over one-third of non-Christian clergy (34%) agree. (Since this group's make-up includes more than four in 10 who self-describe as Christian but do not fall within orthodox Christian beliefs—Mormon, Jehovah's Witness—this explains why such a large number still prefer traditional Judeo-Christian values.)

Faith Leaders' Preferred Standard of Moral Values

% among all clergy

	All clergy	Protestant non-mainline	Protestant mainline	Catholic	Non-Christian
Traditional Judeo-Christian values should be given preference in the US	**66%**	**78%**	**46%**	**68%**	**34%**
No one set of values should dominate the country	**34%**	**22%**	**54%**	**32%**	**66%**

(2014 Clergy, n=1,068)

US Adults' Preferred Standard of Moral Values, 2012 to 2017 (Part 1)

% among US adults

	2012	2015	2017
Traditional Judeo-Christian values should be given preference in the US	**26%**	**27%**	**32%**
No one set of values should dominate the country	**74%**	**73%**	**68%**

US Adults: 2012 (n=1,008), 2015 (n=1,200), 2017 (n=1,019)

These numbers are significant. On one hand, it is unsurprising that clergy feel most loyal to their own value system. But on the other, their desire for preferential treatment appears to challenge the very notion of freedom of religion.

Views among US adults on this question have begun to shifted in recent years. From 2012 to 2017, the proportion of US adults who agree that traditional Judeo-Christian values should be given preference

US Adults' Preferred Standard of Moral Values, 2012 to 2017 (Part 2)

% among US adults

No one set of values should dominate the country

Traditional Judeo-Christian values should be given preference in the US

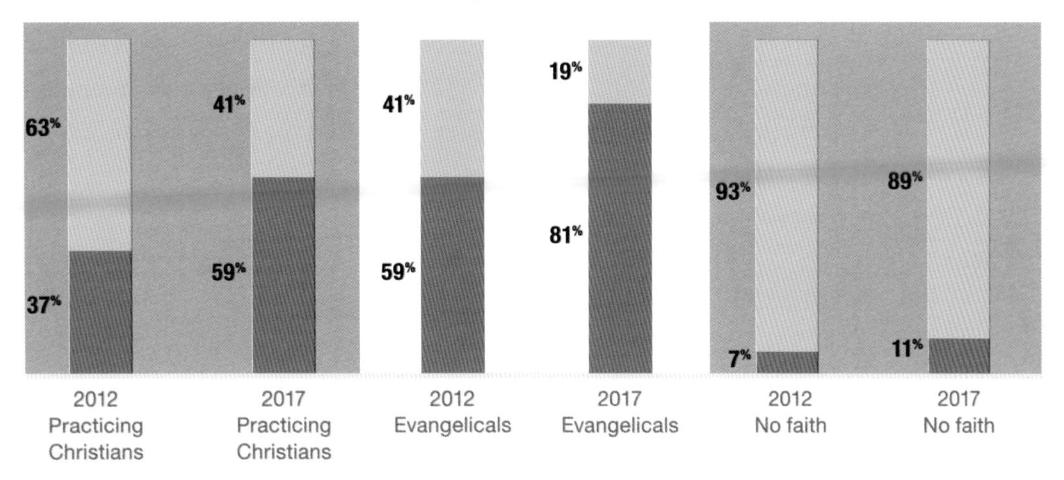

US Adults: 2012 (*n*=1,008), 2015 (*n*=1,000), 2017 (*n*=1,019)

in the US has increased from one-quarter (26%) to one-third (32%). Despite a strong overall preference for neutrality, the tide is beginning to turn in the direction of tribalism.

On a closer look, it appears this tribalistic mentality is most pronounced among Christians (clergy and laypeople). For example, the growth in this view among evangelicals is remarkable: Three out of five (59%) expressed a preference for traditional Judeo-Christian values in 2012, increasing to four in five (81%) in 2017. Evangelicals have been at the forefront of disputes about religious freedom and, as they witness their own value system decline in America, they may be increasingly motivated to see it given preference. The same is true to a lesser extent among practicing Christians. In 2012, almost two in five practicing Christians (37%) believed Judeo-Christian values should be given preference; in 2017 this had climbed to three in five (59%). For comparison, those who do not claim a faith have shifted very little, with most preferring that no one set of values dominates (93% in 2012 to 89% in 2017)—again, pointing to a growing divide between tribes.

We see a smaller but similar movement among US adults when asked whether they would be more likely to support a group that protects the rights of all religions, their own religion or a secular vision of America. While support for the protection of all religions commands a strong majority, there is a measurable shift in those who chose "an organization that protects the rights of those who practice your religion," from 11 percent in 2012 to 17 percent in 2017.

Difficult Conversations

Americans are increasingly likely to want to preserve their own interests and rights

Americans are increasingly likely to want to preserve their own interests and rights. This splintering and polarization of American culture has made it more difficult than ever to reach across cultural divides. Recent Barna research shows that most Americans think it would be difficult to have a natural and normal conversation with minority groups who are different from them. A majority of Americans says they would struggle to have a conversation with a Muslim (73%), a Mormon (60%), an atheist (56%), an evangelical (55%) or someone from the LGBT community (52%).

Evangelicals seem to have a particularly difficult time talking to those outside their group. They report higher tensions than any other group when it comes to having conversations with those who are different from them. For instance, almost nine in 10 evangelicals (87%) believe it would be difficult to have a natural and normal conversation with a member of the LBGTQ community, but only six in 10 in the LGBT community (58%) say it would be difficult to have a natural and normal conversation with an evangelical.

This holds true across the board. Evangelicals consistently report higher levels of difficulty with other groups than those groups report with them. Nearly nine in 10 evangelicals (87%) think it would be difficult to have a conversation with a Muslim, but only seven in 10 of those with other faiths (69%) report difficulty in conversing with evangelicals. Similarly, when it comes to speaking to atheists, 85 percent of evangelicals think it would be difficult, but only two-thirds of atheists, agnostics and those who do not have any faith (66%) say they would have a hard time talking with evangelicals.

Tribalism impairs the connections necessary to a healthy society on even the most basic level

Although evangelicals are most likely to report this difficulty talking to a member of another group, what is most striking is how often a majority of *any* group says it would be hard to have a conversation with *any other* group. Tribalism impairs the connections necessary to a healthy society on even the most basic level.

Viewed through the ministry lens, this suggests it would be helpful for pastors and churches to think creatively about how to develop stronger relationships within their neighborhoods. Churches might organize service-oriented events whose main goal is simply to meet people in the neighborhood surrounding their church—neighborhood block parties, for example. These events could have evangelistic value as well—but if the primary goal is simply building relationships, it might remove some of the fear associated with conversations across religious lines.

Viewed through the relationship lens, individual Christians could try to create non-intimidating spaces for meeting neighbors—perhaps inviting co-workers or neighbors to play board games or other casual activities. Rebuilding social capital requires simple acts that ease the fear and discomfort from interfaith relationships.

Not surprisingly, most groups tend to have more internal than external harmony. For instance, almost three in 10 evangelicals (28%) think it would be difficult to have a conversation with another evangelical. That's a comparatively low number—especially when 87 percent of evangelicals think it would be difficult to have a conversation with a Muslim—but even so points to tension even within groups. This goes beyond evangelicals. Four in 10 LGBT adults (39%) think it would be difficult to have a conversation with another member of the LGBT community. The problem with growing tribalism is not simply that members of individual tribes do not trust other tribes; it's that tribes themselves tend to splinter into subgroups over time, creating ever greater mistrust and isolation.

Difficult Conversations in the Church

Churches ought to be the place where this growing divide is bridged. In a world that increasingly looks at differences as definitions, scripture teaches that all are one in Christ (see Galatians 3:23 and Colossians 3:11).

Most clergy feel at least somewhat prepared to teach their faith community to constructively engage with people who disagree with their views on social issues

The good news is that most clergy (93%) feel at least somewhat prepared to teach their faith community to constructively engage with people who disagree with their views on social issues. Almost two in five (38%) feel very prepared, and a majority (55%) feels somewhat prepared. While still a minority perception, more Catholic clergy (17%) feel not too or not at all prepared; that's four times more than mainline Protestants (4%) who report feeling not too or not at all prepared. Non-Christian clergy are more likely than other pastors to say they are very prepared (56%) to teach their faith community how to engage well in disagreement. This is not surprising, given that adherents to other faiths or no faith often find themselves in the minority in America, at least when it comes to religious self-identification, and thus may have more experience contending for their point of view.

Whether or not they feel very prepared to teach their faith communities to engage constructively on social issues, most clergy agree their congregations want coaching in this area. Almost four in five clergy members (79%) agree that the people in their congregation want help with these kinds of conversations.

How Prepared Faith Leaders Feel to Teach Congregants to Engage Constructively on Sensitive Issues

% among US faith leaders

	All clergy	Protestant non-mainline	Protestant mainline	Catholic	Non-Christian
Very	**38%**	**38%**	**36%**	**31%**	**56%**
Somewhat	**55%**	**55%**	**61%**	**53%**	**40%**
Not too	**6%**	**7%**	**3%**	**15%**	**1%**
Not at all	**1%**	**0%**	**1%**	**1%**	**3%**

2014 Clergy (*n*=1,424)

In the 2015 / 2016 study, Christian clergy were asked how well they feel their congregants are equipped to have difficult conversations about challenging and sensitive social topics. For the most part, very few clergy (7%) believed their congregants were very well equipped. More than half (55%) said they were somewhat well equipped, which was the most common response among clergy from all denominations. But significant numbers (38%) still believed their congregants were not too or not at all equipped. This is noteworthy, especially considering how well prepared clergy feel to teach their congregation to engage in constructive conversation. There appears to be a disconnect here, which likely relates to how comfortable clergy feel about speaking out on certain issues, a problem explored in more detail in the next chapter.

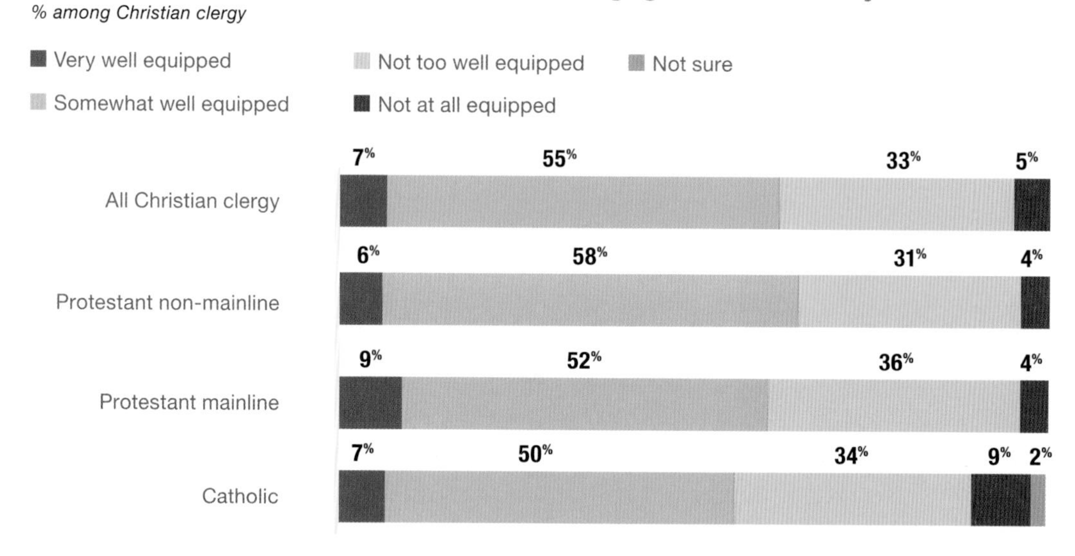

Reaching Across the Divide

Challenging tribalism requires leaders who are willing to reach across the divide and find common ground with groups they have little in common with. The good news is that, based on the 2014 data, more than seven in 10 clergy (72%), regardless of faith tradition, would definitely or probably be willing, in the coming year, to work on religious liberty issues with a local clergyperson of another faith. African American (82%) and mainline Protestants (77%) were more likely than Catholics (70%) or non-mainline Protestants (70%) to say they would definitely or probably be willing to do so.

Small percentages in each segment said they would probably not or definitely not be willing to work with another clergyperson of a different faith. The largest segment among these is non-Christian clergy, one in 10 of whom (11%) reported their strong unwillingness to cross the lines of faith tradition. This is double the proportion of mainline, non-mainline and African American Protestants who said the same.

Barna has found in many instances that positive exposure to those outside one's group leads to increased empathy. As one example, one-quarter of people who spend time with Muslim friends (24%) strongly disagrees that the majority of terrorism is perpetrated by Muslims, compared to just 13 percent among those who do *not* spend time with Muslim friends.

Unfortunately, most Americans do not interact much with those outside their group. In a 2015 study, most people admitted their friends are mostly similar to them in religion, ethnicity, political ideology, socioeconomic group, stage of life, and so on. This kind of tribalism causes people to believe whatever their group believes, regardless of external evidence or opinions to the contrary. Tribalism, then, poses one of the most severe threats in a contested culture, at the very least keeping groups from welcoming one another, let alone learning from each other.

Challenging tribalism requires leaders who are willing to reach across the divide and find common ground with groups they have little in common with

That said, for Christians it also affords an exciting opportunity. For those who share a common faith, there is a chance to embody unity in compelling ways, particularly across racial and political lines—two qualities that should not and must not divide believers in Christ but do often divide ordinary Americans. For example, there is opportunity here, viewed through a ministry lens, for churches to take steps to promote non-white pastoral leadership. Similarly, the biblical call to lift up the poor, to shelter the stranger and to work for the good of the city all offer rich ways to think about solidarity with those who are not Christians.

Viewed through the public square lens, there is opportunity for Christians to partner with people of other faiths or no faith at all to offer aid to the poor and the underserved through joint sponsoring of shelters, food kitchens and so on. There may also be opportunity for supporting local organizations that assist in low-income schools and work with poor children.

In a fractured society, followers of Jesus have two options—to follow the pattern of fracture or to model a better way, embodied through sacrificial love offered to the other

In one of his final editorials for *Christianity Today*, Philip Yancey wrote about the experience of an evangelical friend in one of the poorest neighborhoods in Sao Paulo, a major city in Brazil.

> I recently heard from a friend who visited a barrio in São Paulo, Brazil. He grew nervous as he noticed the foot soldiers of drug lords standing guard holding automatic weapons. They were glowering at him, a gringo invading their turf. "Then the chief drug lord of that neighborhood noticed my T-shirt, which had the logo of a local Pentecostal church. He broke out in a big smile: 'O, evangelicos!' he called out, giving us hugs. Over the years, that church had cared for the children of the barrio, and now we were joyfully welcomed." Some of my friends believe we should abandon the word *evangelical*. I do not. I simply yearn for us to live up to the meaning of our name.[3]

In a fractured society with few common objects of love, followers of Jesus have two options—to follow the pattern of fracture or to model a better way, embodied through sacrificial love offered to the other. The numbers tell an alarming story about America, but they also implicitly suggest that "the harvest is plentiful."

Chapter 3

How Important Is Religious Liberty?

Although religious liberty is an important question facing American clergy, it is a secondary question for most. The Harvard legal scholar Adrian Vermuele notes that issues such as religious liberty are a step removed from the chief issues that concern a people's life together.[4] Before we debate how to resolve our differences, we must first *establish* those differences, which means attending first to what we actually believe about life's ultimate questions and what practices we adopt in response to those beliefs—and only after those issues are resolved turning to questions of how to live together despite our differences. The dominant concern for many clergy is with the first set of questions:

- What are the actual religious beliefs of Americans?
- What do they believe about morality?
- Do they attend church?

Concerns about religious liberty follow from concern about the divisions opening up in America about the great questions of life. In this chapter, then, we review some of these foundational questions that are of such concern to American clergy and offer ways forward for addressing them faithfully in a fragmenting world.

Ministry Concerns

In the 2014 study of clergy, participants were presented with a list of issues that have the potential to affect their ability to minister effectively in the coming decade. Of these possibilities, "teens and young adults dropping out of church" ranked number one among every clergy segment, revealing how common the dropout problem has become. Nearly all Christian ministers and eight out of 10 non-Christian clergy said they were *very* or *somewhat* concerned about this trend.

Concerns about religious liberty follow from concern about the divisions opening up in America about the great questions of life

The second largest concern, cited by nearly two-thirds (65%) of clergy was "the decline of traditional families," followed by a concern over "increasing acceptance of same-sex marriage and LGBT orientations" (55%), "freedom of religion becoming much more limited in the US" (54%) and "Christians remaining faithful and effective as a minority within the US" (53% very concerned). Significantly fewer expressed concern about "minority religions having unequal influence in society in comparison to their size" (28%).

Protestant pastors were given an open-ended opportunity in 2014 to name the two or three cultural or social issues that concern them most. Among the most common answers were LGBT issues (33%); the general spiritual condition of Americans (27%); the decline of traditional families (19%); overall moral decline (14%); poverty and homelessness (14%) and religious freedom (12%). Again we see that the challenges facing clergy are broader than the singular issue of religious freedom. The limitation of religious freedom is a subset of a larger secularizing trend and moral shift away from traditional Christianity.

By a long shot, the challenge of reaching (and losing) younger generations presents the most serious concern of pastors and religious leaders. Young people are coming of age in a culture uncertain about moral and spiritual truth and are deeply distrustful of institutions, particularly the Church—which they are leaving in droves. Barna's most recent research on Gen Z shows that teens 13 to 18 years old are twice as likely as adults to say they are atheist (13% vs. 6%).

Pastors are concerned about the changing nature of the family. Divorce, remarriage, delayed marriage, cohabiting and the rise of single-parent households are changing the nature of the traditional family unit. Christians have long believed that the strength of the family is the strength of a society, and the data shows how children of married couples are economically, mentally and academically better off as they enter adulthood.[5]

This leads to a third concern: broad acceptance of LGBT orientations. The shift in attitudes toward sexual minorities in the last few decades has been dramatic, culminating in the 2015 *Obergefell v. Hodges* Supreme Court decision guaranteeing the right for same-sex couples to marry. Same-sex relationships have become increasingly less taboo, and we've seen a rapid increase in LGBT-inclusive policies in the workplace, in schools and in healthcare. Concerns around LGBT issues are high priority to many clergy and, as explored in the special section on page 59, the two issues of religious freedom and LGBT rights are nearly impossible to separate.

The limitation of religious freedom is likely seen by clergy as a subset of a larger secularizing trend and moral shift away from traditional Christianity

The Future United States

In light of these concerns, if these trends away from Christian morality and church attendance persist, what might the United States look like in the coming decade?

Given a list of possible future scenarios, not all clergy members in the 2014 study agreed on the likelihood of various outcomes. A

Issues that Will Affect My Ability to Minister in the Next Decade

% "very concerned" among US faith leaders

	All clergy	Protestant non-mainline	Protestant mainline	Catholic	Non-Christian
Teen and young adults dropping out of church	72%	74%	73%	77%	55%
The decline of traditional families	65%	76%	36%	75%	44%
Increasing acceptance of same-sex and LGBT orientations	55%	67%	31%	46%	38%
Freedom of religion becoming much more limited in the US	54%	62%	29%	54%	49%
Christians remaining faithful and effective as a minority within the US	53%	59%	44%	38%	
Minority religions having unequal influence in society in comparison to their size	28%	33%	15%	23%	NA

2014 pastors, n=(812)

Current Social Issues of Greatest Concern to Protestant Pastors

% open-ended among Protestant pastors

Issue	%
Homosexual lifestyles / homosexuality / gay marriage	33%
Spiritual condition of Americans / need Jesus	27%
Decline of the family	19%
Moral decline / immorality / lack of personal responsibility	14%
Poverty / homelessness	14%
Religious freedom	12%

(2014 data, open-ended, n=736)

majority of clergy says "society in general will be less moral" (64% very likely)—but they are internally divided. Southern Baptists are the most pessimistic (85%), followed by non-mainline Protestants (77%), mainline Protestants (49%), non-Christians (43%) and Catholics (37%). This divide is not surprising if one assumes that Southern Baptists trend most conservative on these matters, that non-Christians have the least concern about traditional Christian morality and that the remaining groups surveyed basically fall into line somewhere along the continuum between them.

These concerns mirror Barna's other research on morality. We have found that Americans are both concerned about the nation's moral condition and confused about morality itself. Barna's recent *Gen Z* study also found that moral relativism is taking deep root in America.

One-quarter of Gen Z strongly agrees that what is morally right and wrong changes over time based on society, and they are nearly on par with Millennials in believing each individual is his or her own moral arbiter (see p. 55 of *Gen Z*).

Americans are both concerned about the nation's moral condition and confused about morality itself

One outcome, chosen by almost half of all clergy as very likely, is that "Christians will have less influence in society" (46%). At least eight out of 10 in each of the Christian segments believe this is very or somewhat likely; half of non-Christian clergy agree (53%).

It may come as no surprise that the influence of Christianity in the United States is waning. Barna research has observed rates of church attendance, religious affiliation, belief in God, prayer and Bible-reading dropping for decades. Americans' beliefs are becoming more post-Christian and the role and influence of churches are slowly eroding. The reaction to this loss of prominence among Christians is mixed, but how churches respond is vitally important in the days ahead, as Christians move from a dominant culture to a minority culture.

The concerns that follow all relate in some way to the prospect of limited freedoms, religious or otherwise. Nearly half of all clergy (44%) believe that "other kinds of freedoms, not just religious, will also be at risk." There is somewhat more agreement between Christians and non-Christian leaders on this. Two-thirds of non-Christian faith leaders (68%) say this is at least somewhat likely, compared to three-quarters of African American (78%) and mainline Protestants (75%), and nine out of 10 non-mainline Protestants (89%).

Another four in 10 among all faith leaders (41%) say it's *very* likely "the government will have too much control over religious institutions." Nearly half of non-Christian clergy (46%) agree it is at least *somewhat* likely, while half or more of all Christian clergy believe so. Similar proportions predict the likelihood that "people will have less ability to practice their faith without interference."

How Will Diminished Freedom Affect Pastoral Ministry?

Have clergy thought about the possible consequences of restricted religious freedoms for their ministry? The majority of clergy members in the 2014 study had given at least some thought to possible ministry ramifications (77%). About seven in 10 non-Christian (69%) and six in 10 mainline Protestant clergy (61%) said they had done so. These are small majorities compared to the nine out of 10 Southern Baptist pastors who had thought *some* (41%) or *a lot* (49%) about how their ministry might be affected. Other segments fall somewhere between these poles.

A group of ministers who had given at least some thought to how their ministry might be impacted by diminished freedom were given an open-ended opportunity to name these likely effects. The most common answer among one-quarter of clergy (24%) is the likelihood he or she would receive criticism for preaching the truth. Pastors anticipate feeling hesitant to preach, concerned about blowback from a callout culture and broken public discourse.

Pastors anticipate feeling hesitant to preach, concerned about blowback from a callout culture and broken public discourse

The growth in online shaming, attention to microaggressions and debates over political correctness have precipitated a tense battle over language in the US, likely contributing to pastors' fears. One in five foresees the possibility of being pressured or required to perform gay marriages (19%). A loss of tax-exempt status (15%), more difficulty evangelizing (9%) and declines in church attendance and commitment (10%) are other issues clergy fear could be the effects of diminished religious freedom on ministry.

Threats to Religious Freedom

Respondents were invited to rate the threat level of various issues as "not a threat," a "minor threat," a "major threat" or an "extreme threat" to religious liberty. On the whole, a majority of non-Christian clergy do not view the slate of options as particularly threatening to religious freedom. Christian segments, however, demonstrate varying concerns and priorities.

Non-mainline Protestant, Southern Baptist and Catholic clergy have their greatest concerns mostly in common, albeit at varying levels of intensity. These include "religious organizations being required to hire without discrimination toward those in same-sex marriages or same-sex partnerships"; "religious hospitals being required to perform abortions and other services they deem to violate their religious convictions"; and "religious organizations being required to provide health care options they object to" (Catholics and Southern Baptists) or "religious owners of businesses being required to provide services to those with whom they morally disagree" (non-mainline Protestants). A significant majority in each segment views these issues as extreme or major threats.

Issues that Are a Threat to Religious Freedom

% major + extreme threat among US faith leaders who have given thought to the topic

Issue	%
Religious hospitals being required to perform abortions and other services they deem to violate their religious convictions	71%
Religious organizations being required to hire without discrimination toward those in same-sex marriages or same-sex partnerships	66%
Religious organizations not being allowed to operate on college campuses*	65%
Religious organizations being required to provide healthcare options they object to	64%
Religious organizations being sued for termination of employees for things they did in their personal lives that are not consistent with the teachings of their faith	62%
Religious owners of businesses being required to provide services to those with whom they morally disagree	61%
Religious owners of businesses being required to provide healthcare options they object to	61%
Religious organizations on college campuses being forced to accept members who don't adhere to their faith or beliefs	59%
Religious organizations being sued for firing employees who violate faith-based conduct policies	58%
Restricted funding for faith-based universities, schools and other non-profits because of those schools' positions on moral issues	48%
Parents being required to provide standard medical care to their children even if they don't believe in it	32%

* Small sample size

2014 Pastors (n=802)

Mainline Protestant clergy, given their overall greater openness to LGBT relationships, do not share others' concerns about hiring policies with regard to same-sex partnerships—but they do express some concern about the freedom of religious organizations to set faith-based policies. These include requiring religious hospitals to perform abortions or provide morally objectionable services and/or health-care options, and suing religious organizations "for firing employees who violate faith-based conduct policies." These are seen as extreme threats to religious liberty by 20 to 30 percent of mainline Protestant pastors, with greater proportions viewing them as major or minor threats.

African American Protestants share non-mainline Protestant and Catholic concern about hiring policies related to same-sex marriage. But, diverging from other Christian segments, these ministers are more likely to cite "restricted government funding for faith-based universities, schools and other non-profits because of those schools' positions on moral issues" and "religious organizations on college campuses being forced to accept members who don't adhere to their faith or beliefs" as extreme threats to religious freedom.

Enemies of Religious Freedom

Most groups tend to point the finger away from their own group.

But where are those threats emanating from? Are there groups actively trying to negatively impact religious freedom in this country? Here again the evidence of tribalism is apparent. When asked in 2014, at least three-quarters of all clergy (75%) believed atheists or secularists have a negative impact on religious liberty in America. This perception exists across all subgroups of Christian clergy. At the low end, two out of three mainline Protestant clergy (66%) said that secularists have a negative impact on religious liberty. Meanwhile, nearly all Southern Baptists (93%) raised this concern.

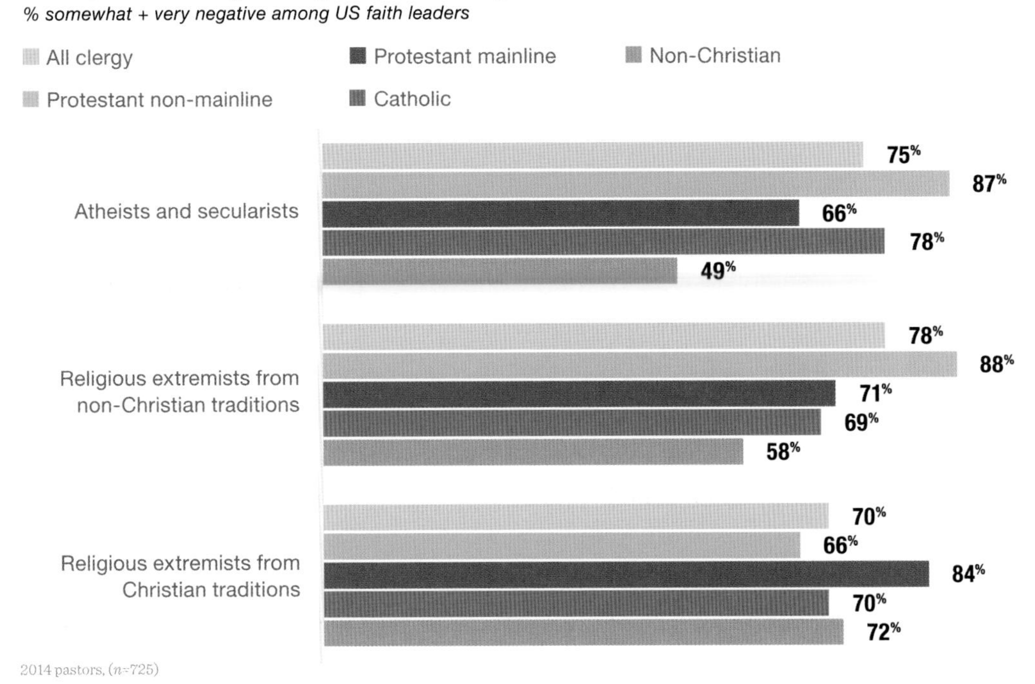

The other culprit commonly cited by clergy as a threat to religious freedom is "religious extremists." But here, again, the tribalized nature of our moment becomes apparent. Nearly nine in 10 non-mainline Protestants say religious extremists from non-Christian religions have a negative impact on religious liberty. According to 84 percent of mainline Protestants, however, religious extremists from *Christian* traditions have a negative impact on religious liberty. This is likely because many, though not all, far-right groups, including white nationalist groups, tend to identify themselves with some form of Christianity.

In other words, most groups tend to point the finger away from their own group. For instance, non-Christian clergy are least likely to believe that religious extremists from *non-Christian* traditions have a negative impact on religious freedom, while also being one of the most likely to say religious extremists from *Christian* traditions have a negative impact. This is true for most traditions, with the exception of mainline Protestants, who are more likely to blame Christian extremists (84%) than non-Christian extremists (71%).

With each group identifying a small group of outsiders as the greatest danger it is easier to discern why some are reluctant to engage in conversation across party lines. Here the public square lens may be a helpful way of viewing the problem. Whatever we think about the religious beliefs of the other group, or their perceptions of our cultural moment, a simple fact unites us: We all must exist within the same country. Thus, it is worthwhile to try to discern where there may be agreement on what constitutes a healthy society and how various groups can work together to realize those shared goals. On this point, it is perhaps worth noting that what seems to most animate both liberals and conservatives is concern about "extremism."

Whatever we think about the religious beliefs of the other group, or their perceptions of our cultural moment, a simple fact unites us: We all must exist within the same country

When it comes to US adults overall, a plurality generally believes religious freedom is becoming more restricted in the US because some groups have actively tried to move society away from traditional Christian values. But that sentiment has shifted over the years. In 2012, about four in 10 (38%) agreed *strongly,* compared to three in 10 a few years later in 2015 (28%) and 2017 (30%). Many of those who previously agreed *strongly* moved to agreeing *somewhat,* meaning that although most Americans do in fact believe some groups have actively tried to move society away from traditional Christian values, they are increasingly less *certain* about whether this is in fact the case. Evangelicals and practicing Christians, who express the highest levels of suspicion toward various groups, have remained fairly stable in their responses since 2012.

On the other hand, in a 2017 study, US adults were asked whether evangelical Christians are actively trying to impose their values on others in the country. Just over half agree (54%). Evangelicals have a complicated reputation in the public eye. Their loyalty to President

Trump despite his decidedly non-Christian behavior and questionable values has confounded many Americans. Evangelical leaders, once known for lamenting moral decay, have thrown their full support behind the president, often defending some of his worst behavior.[6]

Barna also asked whether people believe the LGBT community is

Evangelical Christians Are Trying to Impose Their Values on Others

% among US adults 18 and older

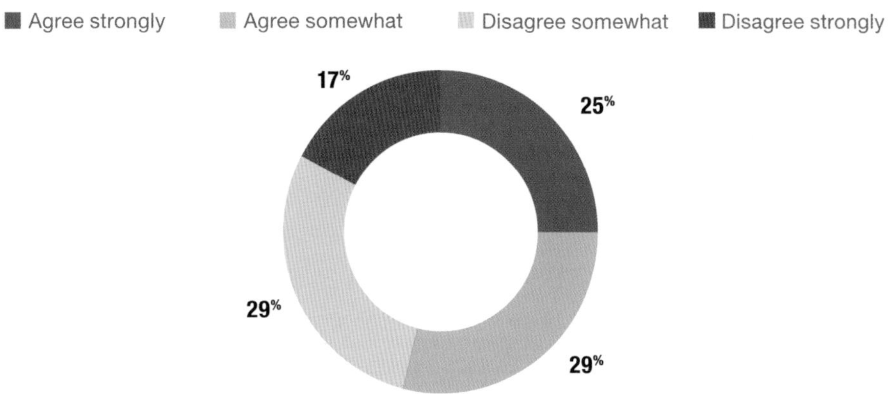

2017 US Adults (n=1,019)

The LGBT Community Is Trying to Remove Christian Values from the Country

% among US adults 18 and older

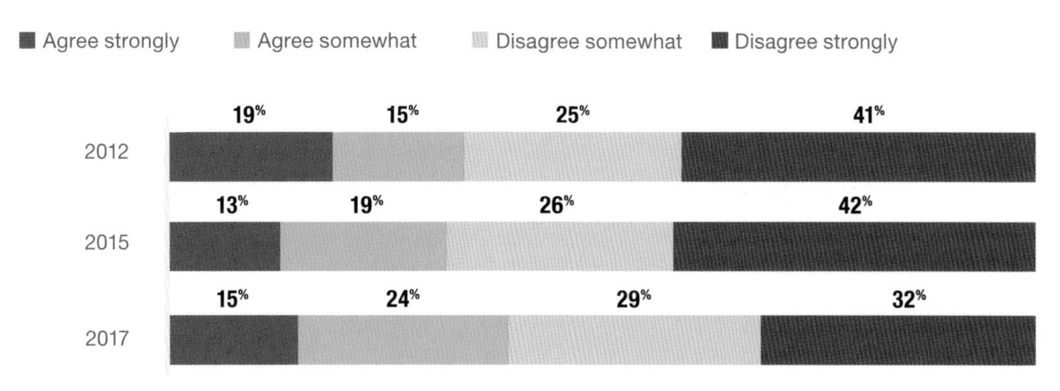

US Adults 2012 (n=1,008), 2015 (n=1,200), 2017=n=(1,019)

trying to remove Christian values from the country—and most consistently disagree.

Evangelicals have a complicated reputation in the public eye

In 2012, only 19 percent agreed strongly, dropping to 13 and 15 percent, respectively, in 2015 and 2017. But interestingly, the same is true at the other end of the spectrum. Two out of five (41%) disagreed strongly in 2012, but that dropped to three in 10 (32%) in 2017. In both cases, the movement has been to the center, with the numbers shifting from *strongly* to *somewhat*, evidence of increasing uncertainty about *who* and *what* is responsible for the shifting tides in American culture.

Despite changes in *strong* agreement and disagreement, overall percentages of those who agree and disagree have not shifted much. In 2012, 34 percent of people believed the LGBT community is trying to remove Christian values from the country. In 2017 that number increased to 39 percent. Conversely, in 2012 two-thirds of US adults (66%) disagreed with that statement, compared to six in 10 (61%) in 2017.

It could be that those for whom same-sex marriage was a preeminent concern have now moved on to other conflicts, or that these changes reflect a generational shift as Boomers give way to Millennials. It could also be that respondents simply perceive other stronger challenges to Christian values. Whatever the explanation of this shift, there remain unresolved tensions between these two tribes.

In the following special section, we focus on questions involving LGBT-related issues. These questions are especially fraught because they incorporate the first-order issues we have already talked about—*What are our religious beliefs? What do we believe about morality?*—and raise specific questions about religious liberty. Viewed through our five lenses, there is perhaps no other set of issues that raises hard questions from all five perspectives.

Special Section

The Church & the LGBT Community

In chapter 2 we noted how loneliness and tribalism actually reinforce one another. When sources of life-giving community fail us, as many Americans feel has happened to them, we quite naturally become more deeply attached to whatever community *does* provide a sense of home and meaning in our lives. This is the backdrop for the conversation. Many in the LGBT community found friendship, love and support with one another when they felt rejected or alienated by broader society—and, often, by Christians and churches.

Thus when clergy want to address questions of gender, sexuality and ethics, they are not simply talking about dos and don'ts as found in their faith's religious texts. They are talking about something deeply personal that concerns a consenting relationship between two adults. Society overall assents to the idea that *consent* is the only word that matters when it comes to sex, so for many people the moral stakes of the issue mostly do not exist—the relationship is simply something to

When clergy want to address questions of gender, sexuality and ethics, they are not simply talking about dos and don'ts as found in their faith's religious texts

be enjoyed. So when people of faith approach these questions, they are approaching a particularly fraught, complex issue in which potential is high for misunderstanding or angry disagreement. No current issue so completely pits modern ideas about human identity against traditional Christian teaching. And it is over this issue that many of the religious freedom debates center. It has become, in many ways, the proxy issue for conflicts over religious liberty.

LGBT Influence & Relationships

It is clear in Barna's research among clergy that LGBT issues are primary in their concerns as ministers. What is the source of this concern? Are clergy in close relationship with members of the LGBT community? Do they minister in neighborhoods where gay and lesbian Americans have significant influence? Are members of the LGBT community attending their churches? All of these factors can influence how clergy think about issues concerning LGBT people.

According to pastors in the 2014 study, most Christian churches (67%) are not located in communities where gay and lesbian Americans have significant influence. Catholic churches (21%) are the least likely to be located in areas of significant LGBT influence, while non-Christian clergy (51%), by contrast, are the most likely to report LGBT influence in the community where their fellowship is located. More than half of mainline Protestant ministers (55%) report openly gay or lesbian attendees to their church, the largest proportion among the Christian segments. As the Protestant mainline has a history of being more welcoming or accepting of LGBT people than non-mainline churches, this is not surprising. Two in five Catholic clergy (40%) say they have openly LGBT attendees at mass. Far fewer pastors in the other Christian segments report openly gay attendees: 22 percent of non-mainline Protestants and 15 percent of Southern Baptists. More than half of non-Christian clergy members (52%), on the other hand, say they have LGBT attendees in their fellowship.

Faith Leaders Who Have Openly LGBT Church Attenders in Congregation

% among US clergy

	All clergy	Protestant non-mainline	Protestant mainline	Catholic	Non-Christian
Yes	34%	22%	55%	40%	52%
No	57%	70%	36%	40%	40%
Not sure	9%	7%	9%	20%	8%

2014 Pastors, (n=820)

Faith Leaders Who Have LGBT Friend or Family Member

% among US clergy

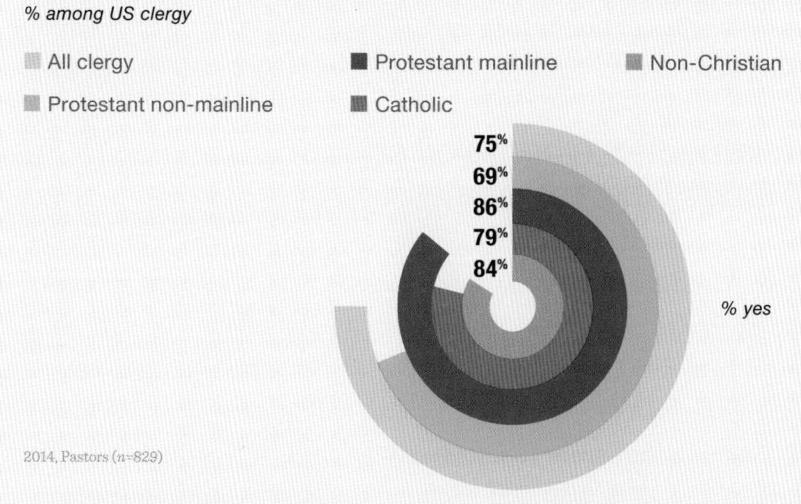

2014, Pastors (n=829)

Compared to the number who report LGBT church attendees, far more pastors in both Christian and non-Christian traditions say they have friends or family members who are LGBT. Eight out of 10 non-Christians (84%), mainline Protestants (86%) and Catholics (79%), and about two-thirds of African American (68%) and non-mainline Protestants (69%) report kinship or friendship with a person who is a sexual minority.

Friendships are a vitally important way to bridge divides and change your perceptions of those who are different to you

Other Barna data has shown that friendships are a vitally important way to bridge divides and change perceptions of those who are different. For instance, those who spend time with Muslim friends are less likely to have prejudicial views toward them. Similarly, strong friendships between LGBT individuals and conservative religious people can help repair some of the mistrust between their tribes. This could also inform the way issues of religious liberty are debated publicly, as in the case of the friendship between LGBT activist Shane Windmeyer and Chick-fil-A CEO and noted evangelical Dan Cathy.[7]

What impact do these relationships have on pastors' understanding of religious liberty? Large majorities of non-Christian leaders (77%), mainline Protestants (68%) and Catholics (63%) say their relationships have had a positive impact on their views. Non-mainline Protestants (50%) are more likely to say their personal relationships with gay friends or family have had no impact on their understanding of religious liberty.

The Impact of *Obergefell* on the Religious Liberty Debate

In 2014 clergy were asked about their position on same-sex marriage. A large majority of most Christian clergy, with a small majority of mainline Protestants (56%), agreed with the statement, "The Church / your faith tradition should hold to its historic position on marriage between one man and one woman." One half of non-Christian clergy (50%) agreed; they were just as likely to prefer the statement, "The Church / your faith tradition should affirm fully monogamous marriage commitments between two people of the same sex" (50%). Forty-four percent of mainline and one in six Catholic faith leaders (16%) also preferred this statement.

One year after this data was collected, the US Supreme Court handed down its decision in *Obergefell v. Hodges*, a landmark ruling requiring all 50 states to perform and recognize same-sex marriage. This

Faith Leaders' Perspectives on Marriage

% among all clergy

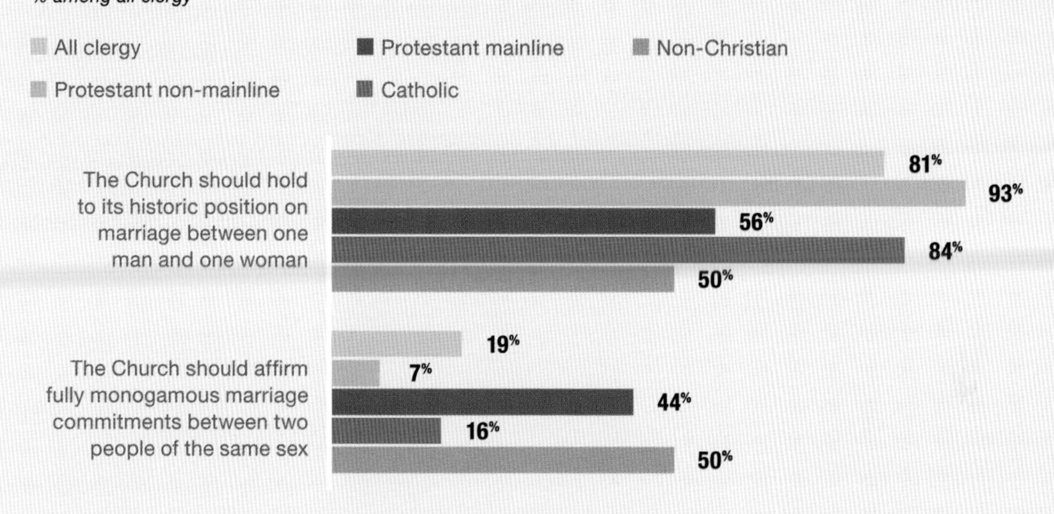

2014 pastors, (n=1,525)

case will be remembered as a major moment in the ongoing debates about religious freedom in the United States.

When the decision was made in 2015, what did people think would be the impact? Based on a poll taken days after the ruling, there was a mixed reception among the American public. Adults were split on whether it would have a more negative (40%) or a more positive impact (37%); one-fifth (19%) said it would have no impact at all.

There was a similar split when it came to people's personal opinions of the decision. Almost half were in favor of the Supreme Court's ruling (48%), while fewer said they were not in favor (43%). Significantly, the survey found almost identical percentages of those *strongly* in favor and those *strongly* not in favor, with both answers accounting for one-third (34%) of responses, leaving the remaining one-third of Americans (32%) somewhere in between the two poles.

Among clergy, the response in the 2015 / 16 poll was telling. Nearly half of all Christian clergy claim that "Christians should resist the same-sex marriage decision and try to find ways of reversing it" (48%).

This is compared to 28 percent who had a more moderate response, claiming, "It is the law of the land and Christians should support it, but explore ways to work around it or diminish its impact within the Christian community." Only 16 percent said, "It is the law of the land and Christians should fully support it." Protestant non-mainline clergy (62%), particularly Southern Baptists (78%), and Catholic priests (53%) were most likely to advocate resistance, whereas almost half of mainline Protestants (46%) said the decision should have Christians' full support.

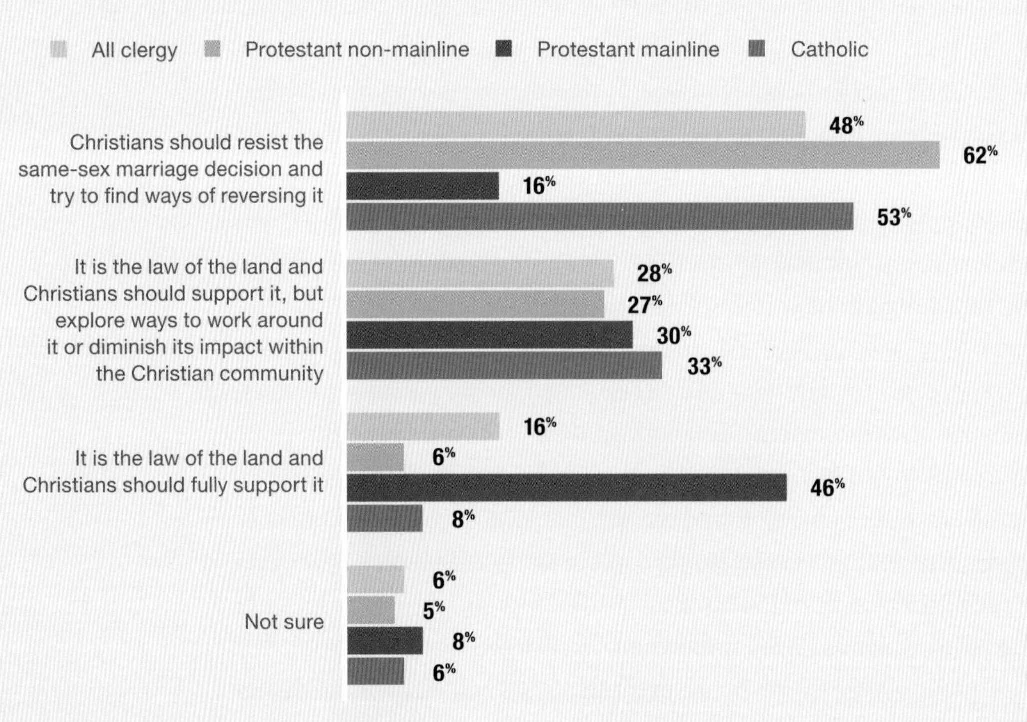

2015/16 Pastors, (n=600)

What's Next?

The biggest question on many minds, particularly for clergy, is *What happens now?* Will they be required to perform same-sex marriages? If so, what will happen to those who refuse to do so? The general public, when asked in 2015, were unequivocal in their view that now that same-sex marriage is legal in the United States, religious institutions should not be legally required to perform weddings for same-sex couples. Eight in 10 said no (79%). This was also the case when asked whether actual clergy members such as priests, pastors and rabbis should be legally required to perform weddings for same-sex couples. The response was the same: Eight in 10 said no (79%).

But what about business owners like bakeries and florists? In the summer of 2018, the Supreme Court heard *Masterpiece Cakeshop v. Colorado Civil Rights Commission* and ultimately ruled in favor of the bakery. This high-profile case focused on a business owner whose religious convictions kept him from baking a cake for a same-sex wedding. The ruling was quite narrow, concerned more with the conduct of the Colorado Civil Rights Commission in this particular case than with broader principles about religious liberty and equal protection under the law. Consequently, it is still very hard to know what the eventual resolution of this particular debate will be.

Public opinion on these sorts of cases is less sympathetic to religious business owners. For instance, almost six in 10 US adults (57%), when asked if they believe business owners who object to same-sex marriage based on their personal religious beliefs should be legally required to offer their services to same-sex weddings, said no. That's 22 points fewer than clergy members who said so. Four in 10 US adults (38%) said that businesses should be required to serve same-sex couples, regardless of the owners' beliefs, nearly double the proportion of faith leaders who said the same.

This tendency to strongly favor the rights of religious groups, but not of business owners, to teach and practice their beliefs is continually reinforced in the data. Nine in 10 Christian clergy (92%) either strongly or somewhat agree that religious groups must remain free to teach and practice the traditional definition of marriage. Catholics (95%) and non-mainline Protestants (95%) are on the same page. Fewer mainline Protestants (81%) agree that churches ought to remain free to teach and practice the traditional definition of marriage. Given that the largest part of the polling differences comes in the group that *somewhat* agrees, it is possible that there is some uncertainty in the Protestant mainline about how to handle the objections of conservative members of denominations who still oppose same-sex marriage.

In fact, mainline Protestants (81%) are just as willing to defend the freedom of religious groups as the general public (81%), a large majority of which believes religious groups should be free to teach and practice the traditional definition of marriage.

Religious Groups Must Remain Free to Teach and Practice the Traditional Definition of Marriage

% among Christian clergy

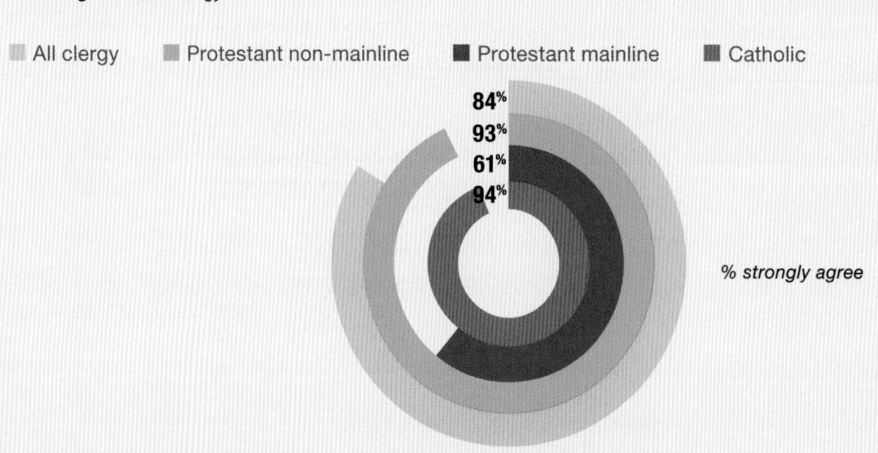

2015/16, Pastors, (n=600)

Addressing LGBT Issues

Moving forward, how well equipped are clergy to deal with the challenges being raised here? Christian ministers were offered a chance to describe in their own words the issues they feel *least* prepared to address when it comes to LGBT people and policies. The five most common issues pastors feel least prepared to address are welcoming without condoning behavior; marriage (traditional covenant vs. civil union); using scripture to teach about sin; how to disciple LGBT people; and the genetic vs. volitional aspects of same-sex attraction. (For a full list of the open-ended responses, please see page 97.)

How Prepared Faith Leaders Feel to Address Questions of Same-sex Marriage and LGBT Issues

% among Christian clergy

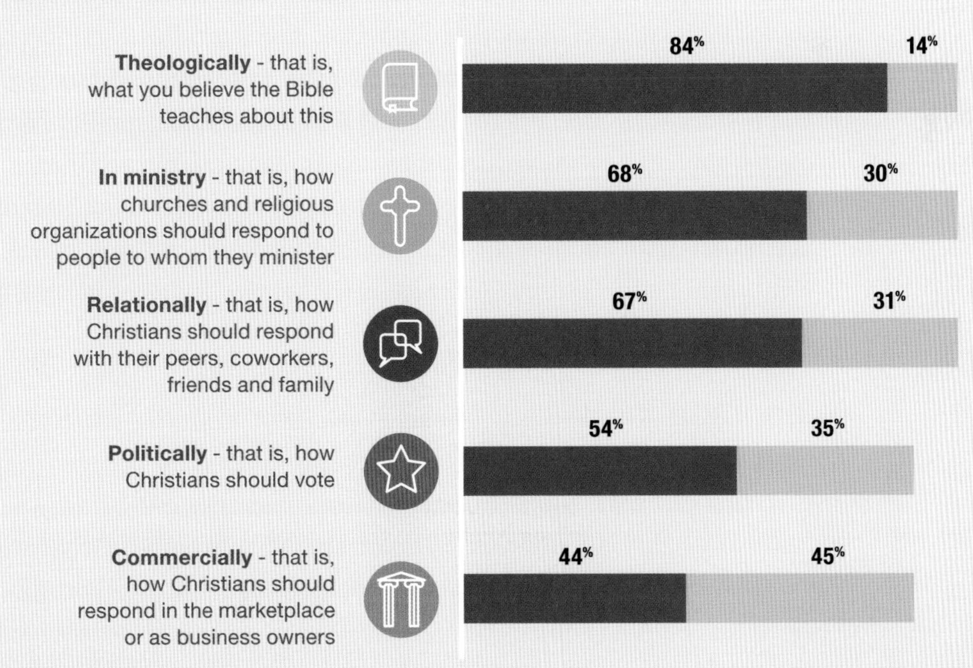

2014 Pastors, (n=1,442)

What makes each of these issues particularly complex is that they incorporate multiple aspects of the five ways to be faithful. For example, the question about marriage is theological—*What does the Bible say?*—but it is also deeply pastoral and concerned with the public square, since marriages are the fundamental social unit of society. Marriage also has political ramifications, so that lens is implicated as well. And, of course, there is a relational component: Do you attend your co-worker's same-sex wedding? How should a religious conservative who affirms the traditional view of marriage but has a child who is married to a same-sex partner reconcile belief with parental love? This is one of the most significant challenges with *many* questions related to LGBT individuals; good responses must account for the ways in which each of the five lenses are connected to the question at hand.

Evaluating their preparedness against a list of areas related to LGBT issues, a large majority of Christian ministers feels at least somewhat prepared to address the issues theologically, in ministry, relationally, politically and commercially. In the realms of theology and politics, mainline Protestants feel less prepared than other segments, but in the relational area they report feeling significantly more prepared. Catholics are less confident than Protestants about their preparedness to address the ministry ramifications of these issues. Non-mainline Protestants feel most prepared theologically, but least prepared commercially.

Incompatibilities

Most Christian clergy (66%) are skeptical that it is possible for Christians to both support civil same-sex marriage *and* affirm the Church's traditional teaching on marriage. This is particularly true among non-mainline Protestants—more than eight in 10 of whom disagree that one can support both (82%). On the other end of the spectrum, the majority of mainline Protestants agree (63%). The general public, based on the 2015 data, tends to side with mainline Protestants, with half (50%) believing that Christians can support legal marriage for same-sex couples and also affirm the Church's traditional definition of marriage. Only one-third (35%) disagree that holding such positions in tension is possible. The view from the outside is simpler, with many believing the Church ought to be motivated by acceptance and belonging, often citing the adage "God is love" to challenge the notion that these two aims cannot be reconciled. This tension is complex, and clergy are immersed within its nuances, so it is unsurprising that they are more skeptical of resolving this tension.

Much work remains to be done in reconciling what appears to many as the conflicting aims of the LGBT community and the Church

Moving beyond same-sex marriage, Christian clergy were asked in 2015 / 16 whether it is possible to advance LGBT rights *and* protect religious freedom. The good news is that half (51%) believe it's possible. The only group more skeptical than not are non-mainline Protestants (54% view these as incompatible), with mainline Protestants being the most optimistic about the possibility (77%). Whatever their view, in a follow-up question, each group felt very certain of those possibilities.

A Permanent Truce

Given the tension between the LGBT community and the Church, is some kind of permanent truce possible? In the most recent poll conducted in 2017, Protestant clergy were fairly evenly split on whether they would favor or oppose federal legislation that ensures protection of both LGBT rights and religious freedom. Most favor this truce (53%), but only slightly more than those who do not (47%). Much work remains to be done in reconciling what appear to many to be the conflicting aims of the LGBT community and the Church.

TO SPEAK OR NOT TO SPEAK?

Clergy members believe it is a critical part of their pastoral role to disciple Christians around social issues. However, when it comes to some issues in particular, clergy feel a level of sensitivity and pressure in how they approach those topics from the pulpit. Nearly three in 10 pastors (27%) admit it has gotten harder to speak from the pulpit about moral and social issues. A divided and often combative American culture makes the stakes high for pastors when they address many of the more potent and controversial issues of our day.

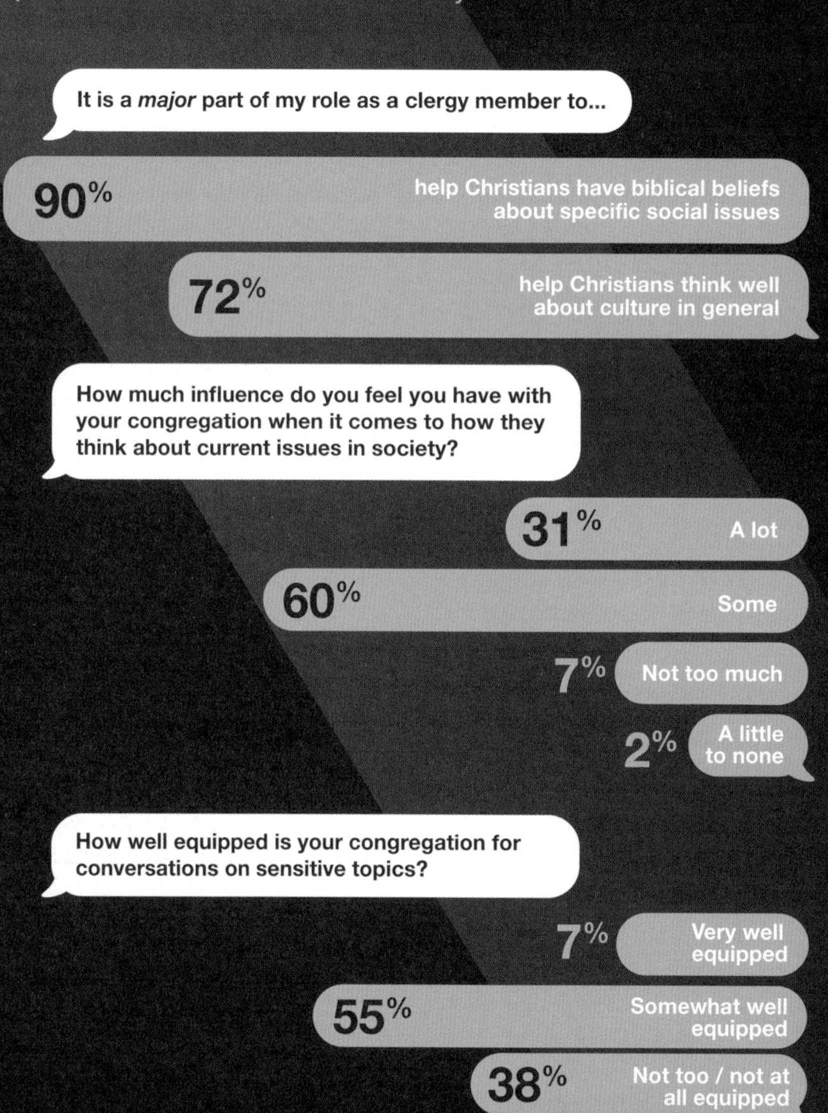

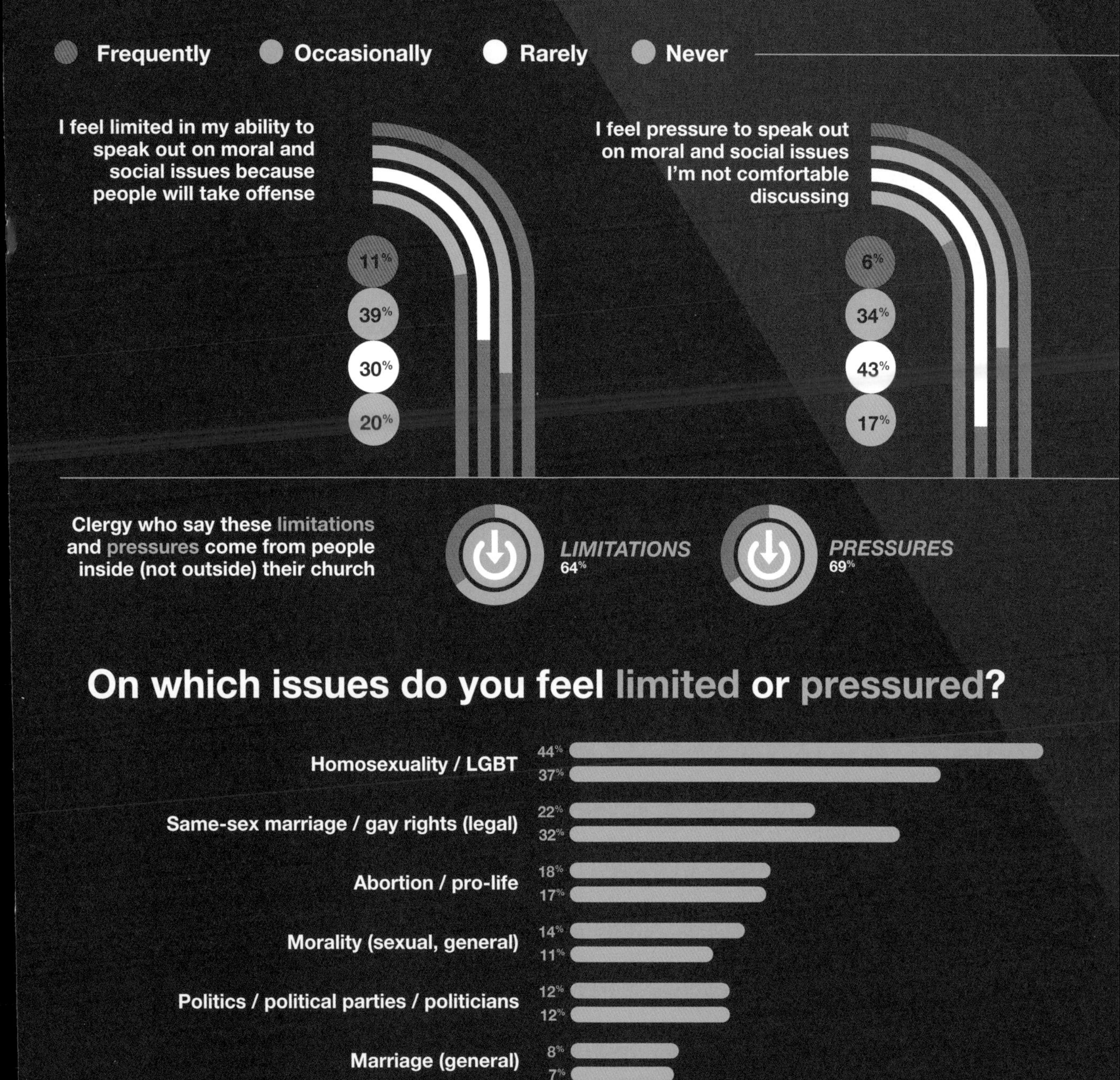

Sex before marriage / promiscuity / cohabitation 7% 10%

Immigration 7% 5%

Religious freedom / church and state 7% 7%

Poverty / social justice 7% 7%

Chapter 4

How Should Clergy Respond?

The goal of protecting religious liberty is not merely to allow individuals to be left alone while they practice their religion. Protecting individual conscience is but part of a framework meant to bring citizens of diverse belief together to construct public life. This requires us to think through another set of questions as we consider the various social problems that have come together in contemporary America:

- How can we think about advocacy for religious liberty in ways that contribute to the common life of a divided society?
- How can religious liberty protections be good news not only for particular religious groups, but for citizens everywhere, regardless of religious belief?

The goal of protecting religious liberty is not merely to allow individuals to be left alone while they practice their religion

Unfortunately, there is a great deal of uncertainty among clergy about what their role is in answering these questions. This chapter explores how pastors see their role in a changing world. There is widespread agreement that American clergy have a uniquely important role to play when it comes to preserving religious freedom in the US. But what precisely is that role? Do pastors feel equipped to lead, or are they feeling uncertain about the future? Many clergy believe it is harder to speak out today than in the past. Why?

The Role of Clergy in Religious Freedom Debates

Barna president David Kinnaman's recent book *Good Faith* reports that the majority of people of faith, even though they feel misunderstood, persecuted, marginalized and extreme in society today, also believe their faith is primarily a positive contribution to society. Large majorities of practicing Christians, and especially Millennials and evangelicals, report two confident attitudes: they feel their faith is a force for good (88%), and that it is essential for society (75%).

This is also true for American faith leaders, a majority of whom believe their position as clergy grants them a unique and important role to play in society. Among clergy from the 2014 study there is widespread agreement that "clergy members have a uniquely important role to play when it comes to preserving religious freedom in the US." In particular, African American clergy (78%) and non-mainline Protestant clergy (72%)—especially Southern Baptists (78%)—have a high view of the their role in this regard. Two-thirds of Catholic (67%) and non-Christian faith leaders (63%), and six in 10 mainline Protestant clergy (61%), agree on their unique role.

For the most part those who don't perceive a unique role for clergy in preserving religious freedom believe they bear the same responsibility as any citizen. It is striking, however, that one in 11 non-Christian

Faith Leaders on Their Role in Preserving Religious Freedom

% among US clergy

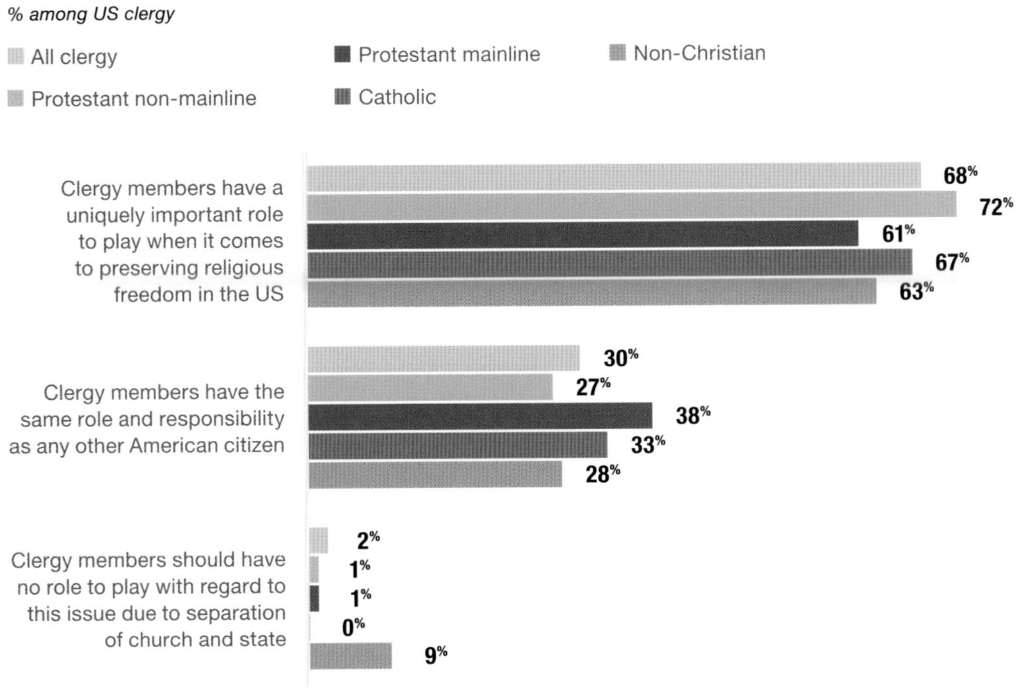

2014 Clergy, (n=1,608)

clergy believes that "clergy members should have no role to play with regard to this issue due to separation of church and state." That percentage is far larger than any other group. Among all Christian segments just 1 percent or less took that view. This may be another instance of tribalism, as Christian clergy are likely to view the separation of church and state in America, a traditionally Christian nation, in ways quite different from how a non-Christian cleric might see it.

So what, exactly, do Christian pastors believe they should do to preserve religious freedom? Christian ministers were offered a list of specific actions related to social and political engagement, and asked whether each action was a major or minor part of their role, or not part of their role at all. Substantial majorities in all denominational

Among clergy there is widespread agreement that "clergy members have a uniquely important role to play when it comes to preserving religious freedom in the US"

segments identified discipleship as their top priority, saying that the major parts of their role are to help Christians have biblical beliefs about social issues, think well about culture in general and understand religious freedom in the US.

Pastors saw themselves as less responsible for direct political and social engagement. Less than half (48%) said defending the rights of other religious groups was a major part of their role. Yet if Christian clergy want to play a principal role in preserving these freedoms, it's important to do so for all people—both as a witness to Christ's servanthood and radical humility and as a purely practical matter. That is, if the First Amendment does not apply equally to all citizens, it is endangered for all citizens, including Christians.

Actions that Are a Major Part of My Role as a Clergy Member

% among Christian clergy

Action	%
Helping Christians to have biblical beliefs about specific social issues	90%
Helping Christians think well about culture in general	72%
Helping Christians understand the nature of religious freedom in the US	65%
Helping Christians to understand their responsibility to vote on specific issues	53%
Defending the rights of other religious groups, even if you disagree with their beliefs	48%
Helping Christians to understand why they should vote for or against specific candidates	21%

2014 Pastors, (n=1,358)

Speaking Out

Helping Christians have biblical beliefs about specific social issues is no easy task. In *Good Faith,* the research reveals that nearly half of non-religious adults perceive Christianity to be extremist. Clergy of all stripes are speaking into a culture that is rife with tension and more contested than ever. The good news is that a plurality of Christian clergy in 2014 felt that speaking from the pulpit about moral and social issues isn't any more difficult than it was five years ago.

Nearly half of non-religious adults perceive Christianity to be extremist

Among Protestant pastors, the difference between 2014 and 2015 / 16 is significant. Those who claimed it was harder dropped seven percentage points from 44 percent to 37 percent in just a year or two. Pastors are feeling that speaking out from the pulpit on moral and social issues that challenge people's thinking and behavior is either no more difficult than it's ever been or actually getting easier.

The minority of clergy members who feel speaking on cultural issues has gotten harder offer a number of reasons for this change. Among the most common are that scripture is viewed as less authoritative;

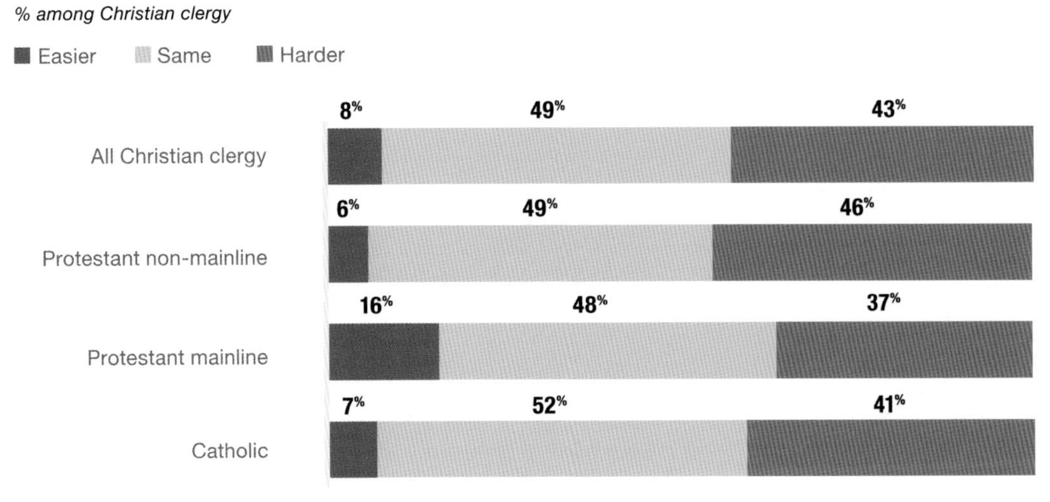

2014 Pastors, (n=1,432)

issues surrounding LGBT people are fraught with emotion; the cultural perception that Christians are intolerant; overall declining morality; a liberal media that seems unfriendly to Christians; the difficulty in finding common ground with people who disagree; and a lack of unity among believers. Unsurprisingly, then, there are close connections between the issues that divide Americans and the issues that clergy find most difficult to address.

Feeling Reluctant to Speak Out

There are close connections between the issues that divide Americans and the issues clergy find most difficult to address

While some Christian pastors believe it is harder than five years ago to speak from the pulpit on moral and social issues, far fewer say they frequently feel *limited* in their ability to do so out of concern people will be offended. In fact, while African American Protestants are the group most likely to say speaking out has become harder (77%), they are least likely, along with Southern Baptists (6%), to say they frequently feel limited in what they can say (8%). Catholic leaders are most likely of all the clergy groups to say they frequently feel limited in their ability to speak out on these issues (13%).

If we look at responses across time, an interesting picture emerges. From 2014 to 2015 / 16, the percentage of Protestant pastors who *never* felt limited dropped by 9 points, while those who *occasionally* felt that way increased by 8 points.

The likeliest explanation for this shift is that between 2014 and 2015 / 16, a number of pastors found that political remarks, which in previous years went mostly unnoticed, were rather suddenly received with some hostility. It is also possible that during that window more clergy had a bad experience on Facebook or Twitter after posting a link or video that might have been seen as unobjectionable in previous years but elicited a stronger response in the current context. As a result, clergy who once felt completely at liberty to speak about political questions felt the need to be more cautious.

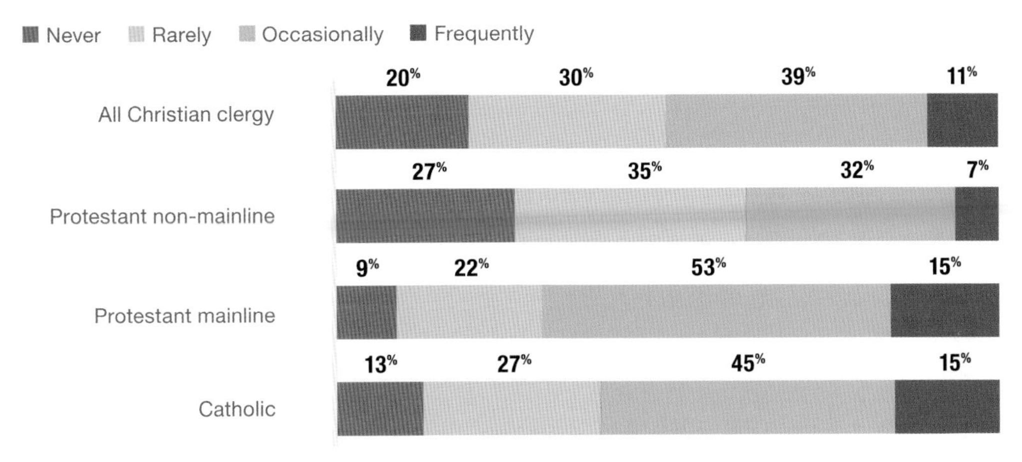

What specific issues cause clergy to feel limited in what they can say? Issues related to sexual ethics and particularly LGBT questions dominated, with 44 percent of Protestant ministers saying they felt limited in their ability to address issues related to homosexuality while 22 percent said the same of same-sex marriage and gay rights. One factor could be that, as LGBT individuals have become fully accepted in common life, some advocates for LGBT rights have also become more confrontational.

Nearly one in five clergy cited abortion as an issue they felt limited in their ability to address. Others cited morality more generally, politics and marriage as limiting issues. Interestingly, religious freedom is further down the list, with only 7 percent of clergy feeling limited in their ability to speak out.

A majority of these same pastors say they worry more about the reactions of those *inside* their faith community (64%) than those *outside* (36%), reflecting both a concern for retaining members as well as

Pastors worry more about the reactions of those inside their faith community than those outside

a pastoral priority of discipleship. Parishioners and members are the primary concern of the pastor, and it is therefore unsurprising that any clergy member would be primarily concerned with those in their own pews.

African American Protestants are an exception: These ministers are divided on which constituency's reaction is of greater concern. This difference has remained steady since 2014, indicating their split concerns are strongly entrenched.

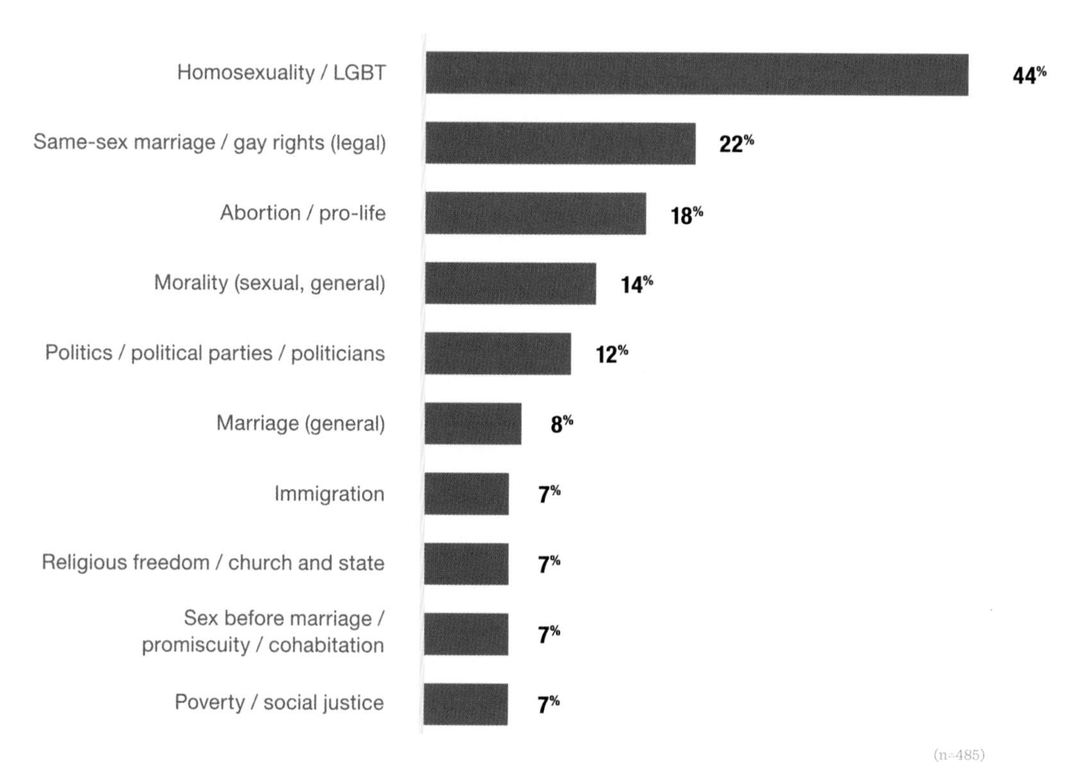

Feeling Pressure to Speak Out

Coming at this question from the other angle, we also asked Christian clergy how often they feel pressured to speak out before they're ready to do so. A majority in every denominational segment rarely, if ever, feels that kind of pressure. Those in each segment who frequently feel pressured are a similar proportion to those who frequently feel limited.

These pastors feel pressured to address a variety of issues. Perhaps ironically, the five most popular are the same issues on which some pastors feel *limited* to speak about—signaling the great tension they are living with in these areas. Specifically, they list LGBT people, orientations and identities; same-sex marriage and gay rights; abortion; sexual morality; and political parties, candidates and policies. Again, pressure to speak about religious freedom is low on the list.

What this data likely tells us is that not only is America fragmenting, churches are as well. The result is that pastors ministering in more

How Often Pastors Feel Pressure to Speak Out Before They Are Ready

% among Christian clergy

	All clergy	Protestant non-mainline	Protestant mainline	Catholic
Frequently	6%	5%	6%	11%
Occasionally	34%	30%	38%	44%
Rarely	43%	44%	42%	38%
Never	17%	20%	14%	7%

2015 / 2016 Pastors, (*n*=601)

politically diverse churches will feel squeezed on both the right and the left while ministers in more politically homogeneous churches will feel pushed further and further toward the consensus of their particular congregation. Both pastoral independence and political centrism could be casualties of these trends.

Although they're most concerned about the reactions of those *in* their faith community, pastors are more likely to feel pressure from people *outside* their church to speak out on cultural issues. For example, two out of five non-mainline Protestant ministers (40%) say that,

Issues Pastors Feel Pressured to Speak About

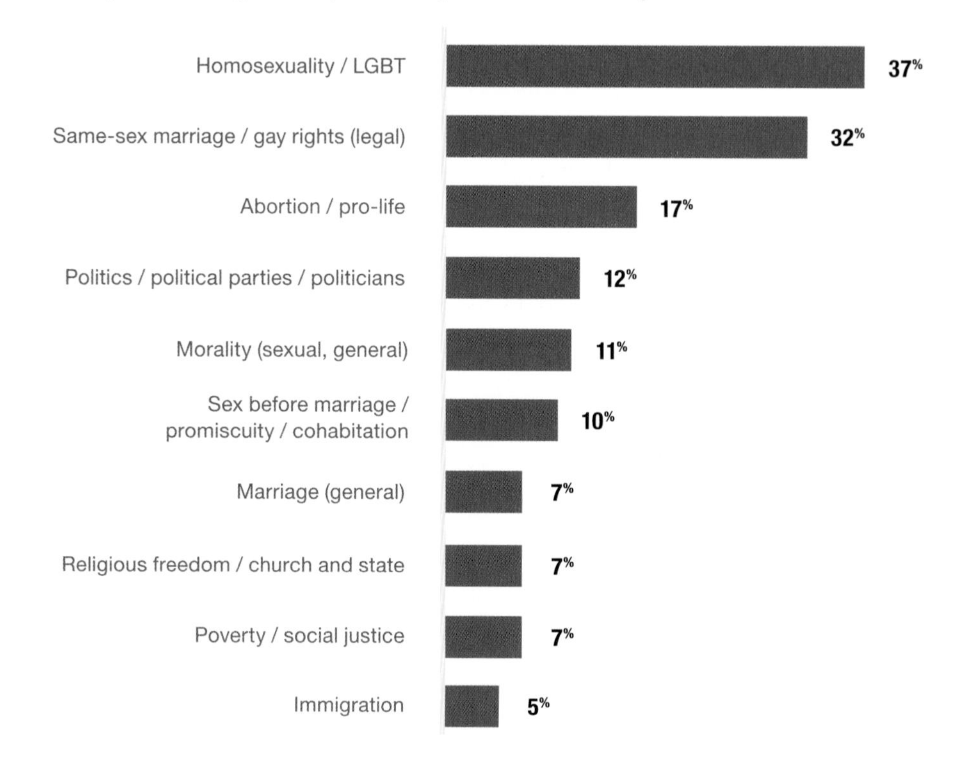

2014 Pastors, (n=524)

were they to speak out on moral issues, they feel more concerned about the reactions of people outside their church than inside. But three out of five non-mainline pastors (59%) say they also feel pressure to speak out from people outside their church, rather than from those inside.

This shifted significantly from 2014 to 2015 / 16. Those clergy who feel pressured from inside their church to speak out on cultural issues that they're not ready or not comfortable discussing rose from 44 percent to 69 percent, a marked rise in a short period. Clergy are clearly feeling a great amount of pressure to speak into some of the most controversial issues of the day and, looking at the data above, it's clear that those are mostly LGBT issues. These points of cultural tension continue to be the battlegrounds for religious discourse in America.

Clergy are clearly feeling a great amount of pressure to speak into some of the most controversial issues of the day

Being Good Neighbors

There is a lot of work to be done by both clergy and ordinary American citizens if we are to rebuild public trust between neighbors and between citizens and institutions. Even small steps will require that religious leaders and people of faith take up an understanding of religious liberty that is not chiefly concerned with protecting their right to practice their religion without being bothered, but that instead sees in religious liberty the opportunity to freely serve one's neighbor according to conscience.

The goal of religious liberty is not to exacerbate tribal divisions by protecting the rights of groups to discriminate against each other. The goal is, rather, to strengthen the whole political community by preserving space in which people can freely serve one another as neighbors. If we are to see a change in tribal isolation, it will be because we learn to reorient our concerns for religious freedom away from our own needs and toward our neighbors.

Leading with Humility, Discernment & Courage

As we look to the future of faith in the United States, effective faith leadership requires humility, discernment and courage. We need humility to see our own blind spots and the experience of others, discernment to know how to think and act, and courage to bring faith into the public square—but also courage to accommodate others' religious freedom.

The late pastor and missionary Francis Schaeffer once preached a sermon called "No Little People." There he argued that Christians often mistakenly see their work as small and insignificant and, because of this wrong perception, end up chasing after stations in life that are actually unhelpful to them and unhelpful to the advancement of the gospel.

> Jesus commands Christians to seek consciously the lowest room. All of us—pastors, teachers, professional religious workers and non-professional included— are tempted to say, "I will take the larger place because it will give me more influence for Jesus Christ." Both individual Christians and Christian organizations fall prey to the temptation of rationalizing this way as we build bigger and bigger empires. But according to scripture, this is backward: We should consciously take the lowest place unless the Lord himself extrudes us into a greater one.[8]

There is something here that relates to the religious liberty debates. The temptation for Christian leaders is to say that religious liberty must be upheld chiefly for our own benefit. This may merely come from a self-preservation mindset—to ensure one's individual church or religion can be kept safe, with less regard for other religions. At worst, such temptations lead people of faith to approach the religious freedom question in a way that actually deepens partisan divides in America. But if we see religious liberty as a blessing not only for Christians but for society as a whole, then we may be on our way toward a healthier relationship to this issue in particular and to society more generally.

In the Gospels, Christ says that those who wish to be great in God's kingdom will be servants—and not merely servants of great lords, but servants of all people. The debate about religious practice and common life in the United States must be seen, then, not chiefly as a debate about how a shrinking church can stage a rear-guard action to protect its social standing. It must rather be framed in terms of how Christians can advocate for policies that allow Americans to freely offer their talents, time and service to one another in keeping with their conscience. If we can make the appeal on this ground, then we may not only achieve a narrow political victory, but will also honor the God whom Christians worship—a God who, after all, poured out his own life for the sake of the world.

To make this more practical, we might return to the idea of the five lenses—five ways we can embody humility, discernment and courage—and ask what specific actions Christians should be taking on each front in this particular cultural moment. To review, the five lenses are:

- **Theology:** What do God's word and the church's wisdom reveal about this?
- **Ministry:** What is the proper pastoral response to people living in a fallen world?
- **Relationships:** How should I engage friends and neighbors with whom I disagree?
- **Politics:** What government policies, however imperfect, best empower human flourishing?
- **Public Square:** What is the appropriate relationship between personal conviction and day-to-day interactions with those who hold different beliefs?

Theology: *What does God's word and the Church's wisdom reveal about this?*

The first lens is theological, reflecting Christians' perpetual need to return both to the truths of the faith handed down in scripture and to a basic delight in God's goodness and the joy of centering ourselves upon these truths; to know and contemplate truth is a good thing in itself. Yet today, many issues that are front and center in the public conversation have exposed deep theological differences, which is one reason the debates cause such angst both within the Christian community and outside of it. Interpretations of scripture differ from church to church and from denomination to denomination.

This is, of course, why religious liberty exists: to protect the rights of people with varying religious beliefs to practice those beliefs. People of faith can look through a theological lens to view any manner of public and private activity: from abortion, to immigration, to capital punishment, to same-sex marriage. And they should continue to probe scripture for guidance on every issue, to seek theological discernment from Church history and governing church bodies, to meet in community with other believers and faith leaders to weigh these matters together. Living peacefully in a pluralistic society does not require unpopular theology to be abandoned. Rather, it demands continuing, prayerful investigation into the issues people are questioning most. Barna's research shows that Christians generally desire thoughtful exegesis and sound theology to help them parse the overwhelming onslaught of opinions and information they face, from social media to political forces. While theological discernment may lead to socially unpopular opinions, pastors and spiritual leaders are called to help those they lead live effectively as countercultural examples.

Yet Barna's studies have also revealed that "judgmentalism" and "hypocrisy" are among the top negative perceptions of the American church. Such perceptions often arise from Christians' attempt to focus a theological lens onto any and all interactions with non-Christians. We know as Christians that conviction to follow God's laws—and the will to do so—come from the grace of the Holy Spirit. To demand that nonbelievers conform to those laws without a conversion to Christianity and the transforming work of the Spirit is to violate their religious freedom.

Ministry: ***What is the proper pastoral response to people living in a fallen world?***

Perhaps you have heard the quote (attributed to various people), "Be kind, for everyone you meet is fighting a battle you know nothing about." For faith leaders, this is perhaps at the heart of one's calling to ministry: to faithfully walk alongside people through crisis and orient them toward the God of healing, redemption and love.

Viewing religious liberty issues through the ministry lens, therefore, requires a level of empathy and attunement to the personal battles people are fighting. Stating the "correct orthodox thinking" may do little to comfort a young man struggling with his sexuality who is wondering if God really loves him or if he will ever be able to have love in his lifetime. To truthfully cite the biblical reasons for being pro-life without discernment or humility may ring hollow in the ears of the expectant single mother with a minimum-wage job and no family support. In other words, our theological convictions must be tethered to a compassionate understanding of the real-world people to whom we hope to minister.

The on-the-ground view pastors have on these issues is invaluable; personal encounters take "issues" out of the abstract and into the embodied. Theology centers our belief on the historical and orthodox, but ministry channels those beliefs through empathy and love as we confront a flesh-and-blood person, as we interact with fellow image-bearers around us.

Christian leaders understand the issues facing their congregants: depression, heartache, economic uncertainty, questions of sexuality, loneliness, and so on. As we've seen in this report, such personal issues are at the forefront of pastors' concerns. At its core, being a faith leader is to care for people. Religious liberty issues may often seem structural, systemic, institutional—not the sort of thing that occupies the reality of shepherding real people. But many of the concerns central to religious liberty *do* have an impact on the lives of individuals: from parents to school teachers to nonprofit and business leaders. The ministry lens allows you to help individuals, families and communities wrestle with systemic issues that affect their lives.

Relationships: *How should I engage friends and neighbors with whom I disagree?*

Relationally, there are two temptations Christians are likely to face in this cultural moment. The first is to point people to facts about an issue without taking time to ask questions, empathize and understand their neighbor. At a minimum, this approach will come off as indifferent and cold.

The other temptation is the opposite error, which is to work so hard to show compassion and to listen that we never get around to offering people hope found in Christ. The need, then, is for Christians to be mature, wise neighbors who can both express sincere interest in and affection for others while also being secure enough to communicate the gospel with respectful confidence.

At Barna, recent research shows a growing discomfort with spiritual conversations. A fear of offense or of coming across as judgmental often drives such discomfort. In a pluralistic society, tolerance and a "you do you" perspective can put a wet blanket on difficult conversations. These may be valuable postures when speaking with strangers or mere acquaintances—people with whom we have not built the trust necessary for more vulnerable or complex conversations.

Cultivating the right mix of loving boldness and countercultural kindness lies at the heart of relationally vibrant Christian witness. For spiritual leaders, and for Christians in general, the aim must be to build deeper friendships with those who are different from us. There is little value in shouting from a soapbox to those who do not trust our voice, but there is equally little value in simply "preaching to the choir" and only having difficult conversations with those who think just as we do. As this report shows, evangelicals in particular struggle to make friends with and talk to those who are different from them. Yet fostering relationships with those outside our tribe is essential and can lead to more empathy (on both sides) and to opportunity for gracefully and gently sharing our perspectives on contentious issues. The research shows clearly that Christians—and faith leaders, too—are hungry for this kind of conversational, relational preparedness.

Politics: *What government policies, however imperfect, best empower human flourishing?*

Politically, the biggest need is to make sure our arguments for religious liberty do not collapse into an argument for privatizing religious faith in the same way other sources of meaning or conviction have become privatized in recent years. If we argue for religious liberty purely on grounds that we need to be left alone, then we're just another party in the fragmentation of the United States—another tribal group wanting to protect its right to pull away from other tribal groups. On the other hand, if we can make the case for religious liberty as a positive social value for all people, then we are on the right track.

In part, this requires a true reckoning with what laws are "those of the land" and which are specific to our religious context. At times this distinction may seem clear. Religious observance of diet, for instance, has not become a cultural fracture. Yet so often those lines are blurred. When spiritual leaders consider which political issues to speak out on, it's important to be certain those issues are a universal good for human flourishing and not a matter of personal discipline, spiritual transformation or church community.

Humility is a vital political virtue in such times. Christians have not always gotten it right when it comes to politics; we have often been wrong. We see only through a mirror darkly, this side of heaven. We must be willing to listen closely to those who disagree with us, consider their political opinions seriously and take our uncertainties to God when they arise.

Public Square: *What is the appropriate relationship between personal conviction and day-to-day interactions with those who hold a different set of beliefs?*

Finally, as faith plays itself out in the public square—matters of institutions and businesses, neighborhoods and communities, and public discourse—we must enter these arenas with an awareness of the cultural landscape. The isolation brought about by tribalism causes members of one tribe to find it very hard to believe in the goodwill of another. But this must not be an excuse for people of faith who exercise humility, discernment and courage. Christians should be, in the words of Jesus, innocent as doves and wise as serpents, alert to both the need for kindness in the public square and also the rhetorical challenges involved in working for a revitalization of the good in our public square.

The pressure to satisfy everyone on all sides, and to avoid offense, is very real today, especially in the digital era. The public nature of social media allows for all to see our slip-ups and inconsistencies. The "outrage machine" devours many organizations for what often seem like minor missteps—and this policing happens on both sides of the political aisle and in all facets of the theological spectrum. The stakes are high in the public square.

As the research reveals, the issues pastors feel most pressured to speak out on are the same ones they feel limited to speak on. The pressure squeezes from all corners: those demanding that the church take a stand and those outraged when it does (or outraged when that stance is other than what they'd hoped). As challenging as it may be, faith leaders must be committed for the long haul, educating and equipping their people to respond with love and conviction, in word and deed. This, after all, is the essence of discipleship.

• •

The fabric of our social conversation about religion may be breaking apart—in fact, that's the image our designers meant to convey on the cover of the report you're reading! Yet, this fragmentation provides opportunities for people of faith in contemporary America. Faith leadership in a divided culture is complex and challenging but affords many opportunities for the cause of the gospel.

In every facet of that leadership, humility, discernment and courage are key. Humility to learn from others, to know *when* to speak and *what* to speak. Discerning how to minister to those who are facing real difficulties. The right kind of courage that connects empathy to difference-making conviction. Yet these practices do not happen in a vacuum—that is to say, they do not happen alone. To discern our way forward, Christian leaders can talk to one another about the tough issues, seek historical and contemporary guidance, fall on our knees in prayer together, and seek God's heart and the direction of the Holy Spirit.

Appendix A

Methodology

Throughout this book we refer to primary research that is not footnoted. These statistics and data-based analyses are derived from a series of national public-opinion surveys conducted by Barna Group.

Once data was collected, minimal statistical weights were applied to several demographic variables to more closely correspond to known national averages. On questions for which tracking was available, findings from these recent studies were compared to Barna's database of national studies from the past three decades. Data from the clergy study were minimally weighted on denomination and region to more closely reflect the demographic characteristics of churches in each media market.

When researchers describe the accuracy of survey results, they usually provide the estimated amount of "sampling error." This refers to the degree of possible inaccuracy that could be attributed to interviewing a group of people that is not completely representative of the population from which they were drawn. For the general population surveys, see the table on the next page for maximum sampling error.

Sponsor	Dates		Collection method	Sample size	Sampling error*
Maclellan	July 2014	Faith leaders, Christian and non-Christian clergy	Telephone and online	**1,608**	**±2.2**
Maclellan	December 2015-January 2016	Protestant pastors and Catholic priests	Online	**602**	**±3.9**
Maclellan	April 2017	Protestant pastors	Online	**601**	**±3.9**
Inspiration Network	May 2008	US adults	Telephone	**1,003**	**±2.9**
Mark Rodgers	November, 2012	US adults	Telephone	**1,008**	**±2.9**
American Bible Society	February 2015	US adults	Online	**1,000**	**±2.9**
Alliance Defense Fund	September 2015	US adults	Telephone and online	**1,200**	**±2.7**
Barna	June 2015	US adults	Telephone	**1,011**	**±2.9**
Barna	July 2015	US adults	Online	**1,237**	**±2.6**
Barna	July 2016	US adults	Online	**1,097**	**±2.8**
Barna	August 2015	US adults	Online	**1,000**	**±2.9**
Barna	August 2015	US adults	Online	**1,000**	**±2.9**
Barna	October 2017	US adults	Online	**1,019**	**±2.9**

*percentage points; sampling error reflects a 95-percent confidence level.

LGBT Issues Pastors Feel Least-Prepared to Address

% among Christian clergy

	All Christian	All Protestant	Catholic
Marriage (traditional vs. civil unions)	8%	6%	12%
Balance between loving and welcoming them without condoning their lifestyle	7%	8%	2%
Using Scripture to defend that it's a sin (when it's accepted by society)	6%	7%	3%
How to interact with and disciple them	4%	5%	2%
"I was born this way" / genetic and scientific aspects	4%	4%	1%
Overcoming the hatred shown them by the church / help congregation to love	4%	5%	3%
How to understand them	4%	5%	2%
Membership / what roles they should play in church / ordination	3%	3%	3%
Transgender	3%	4%	3%
Congregation is divided on the issue	3%	4%	3%
Adoption / impact it has on families	2%	2%	5%
Christian perspective automatically viewed as intolerant	2%	3%	1%
Legal ramifications	2%	2%	2%
Uncomfortable / complex topic / don't want to discuss / don't know what to say	1%	1%	2%
Monogamy / their desire for happiness and love	1%	1%	3%
Political pressure / agendas	1%	1%	-
Other	10%	9%	15%
Don't know	7%	8%	7%
None / I feel prepared	36%	34%	39%

2014 Pastors, Christian clergy (*n*=1,252), 2014 Pastors, Protestant (*n*=936)

Appendix B

Glossary

Clergy segments

All Clergy: all leaders (Catholic, Protestant, and non-Christian faith) included in the study

Non-Christian Clergy: Leaders of religious groups that do not identify as Christian, such as Jewish rabbis, Muslims, Hindu, Buddhist, and other religious faith leaders. Mormon and Jehovah's Witness faith leaders are also included in this category, including those who identify as "Christian."

Protestant Mainline Clergy: Pastors from Protestant denominations such as American Baptist Churches USA, the Episcopal Church, Evangelical Lutheran Church of America, United Church of Christ, United Methodist Church and Presbyterian Church USA

Protestant Non-mainline Clergy: Pastors from Protestant traditions such as charismatic / Pentecostal churches, the Southern Baptist Convention, churches in the Wesleyan-Holiness tradition, and non-denominational churches not included in mainline

Catholic Clergy: Leaders of Catholic or Roman Catholic churches

Protestant Pastor: Pastors who are not part of Catholic or non-Christian faith

African American Protestant Pastor: Pastors from Protestant traditions who lead primarily African-American churches, most (92%) of which are African-American themselves.

US Adult segments

Evangelicals: Evangelicals have made a personal commitment to Jesus Christ that is still important in their life today and believe that, when they die, they will go to heaven because they have confessed their sins and have accepted Jesus as their Savior (Barna's "born-again" criteria) and meet seven other conditions: say their faith is very important in their life today; believing they have a personal responsibility to share their religious beliefs about Christ with non-Christians; believing that Satan exists; believing that Jesus Christ lived a sinless life on earth; asserting that the Bible is accurate in all that it teaches; believing that eternal salvation is possible only through grace, not works; and describing God as the all-knowing, all-powerful, perfect deity who created the universe and still rules it today. Being classified as an evangelical is not dependent on church attendance or the denominational affiliation of the church attended. Respondents are not asked to describe themselves as "evangelical."

Practicing Christians are self-identified Christians who strongly agree their faith is very important in their life and have attended a worship service within the past month or more.

No Faith are atheists or agnostics, or people who choose "none of the above" from a list of religious affiliations.

Generations

Elders born before 1946
Boomers born between 1946 and 1964
Gen X born between 1965 and 1983
Millennials born between 1984 to 1998
Gen Z born between 1999 and 2012

Appendix C

Notes

1. Moore, Russell. "Religious Liberty for All." https://erlc.com/resource-library/articles/religious-liberty-for-all
2. Putnam, Robert. *Bowling Alone.* New York: Simon and Schuster, 2000.
3. Yancey, Philip. "O, Evangelicos!" *Christianity Today,* https://www.christianitytoday.com/ct/2009/november/28.65.html'
4. https://thejosias.com/2018/07/19/according-to-truth/
5. Barna Group. "Who is Gen Z?" https://www.barna.com/who-is-gen-z/
6. https://www.theatlantic.com/magazine/archive/2018/04/the-last-temptation/554066/
7. https://www.huffingtonpost.com/shane-l-windmeyer/dan-cathy-chick-fil-a_b_2564379.html
8. Francis Schaeffer, "No Little People," *The Complete Works of Francis Schaeffer,* vol. 3 (Wheaton, IL: Crossway Books, 1982).

Appendix D

Acknowledgments

The research for this study was coordinated by Brooke Hempell with foundational analysis by Cory Maxwell-Coghlan and Doug Brown, and data verification by Pam Jacob. Jake Meador wrote and edited the report, with direction from Roxanne Stone. Doug Brown proofread the manuscript. Kate Turnbull designed the cover and infographics, and Annette Allen designed interior layout. Brenda Usery managed production. Jennifer Hamel and Mallory Holt coordinated as project managers.

Additional thanks for the support of our Barna colleagues: Amy Brands, Daniel Copeland, Bill Denzel, Aly Hawkins, Raven Hinson, Traci Hochmuth, Savannah Kimberlin, David Kinnaman, Steve McBeth, Jess Villa, Todd White and Alyce Youngblood.

About the Project Partners

Barna Group is a research firm dedicated to providing actionable insights on faith and culture, with a particular focus on the Christian Church. Since 1984, Barna has conducted more than one million interviews in the course of hundreds of studies, and has become a go-to source for organizations that want to better understand a complex and changing world from a faith perspective.

Barna's clients and partners include a broad range of academic institutions, churches, non-profits and businesses, such as Alpha, the Templeton Foundation, Fuller Seminary, the Bill and Melinda Gates Foundation, Maclellan Foundation, DreamWorks Animation, Focus Features, Habitat for Humanity, The Navigators, NBC-Universal, the ONE Campaign, Paramount Pictures, the Salvation Army, Walden Media, Sony and World Vision. The firm's studies are frequently quoted by major media outlets such as *The Economist*, BBC, CNN, *USA Today*, the *Wall Street Journal*, Fox News, *Huffington Post*, *The New York Times* and the *Los Angeles Times*.

www.barna.com

For 75 years, **The Maclellan Foundation** has been making financial investments to help Christians thrive, both in the US and around the world. The Foundation's leaders believe shifting cultural dynamics have put First Amendment rights under considerable pressure—an urgent issue not only for Christians, but for all Americans—and that this research can help us better understand the stakes and the possible solutions. The Maclellan Foundation is pleased to partner with Barna Group to sponsor this important research on our shared religious freedoms.